Black Women IN BUSINESS

JOURNEYS IN RESILIENCE

ROSE SMITH AND DEBORAH COLE

Authors: Rose Smith and Deborah Cole.

Websites:
blackwomeninbusiness.org
deborahcoleconnections.com

Photography: All photos are by Deborah Cole unless otherwise specified
Cover and Interior Design: Victoria Wolf, wolfdesignandmarketing.com.
Publishing Services: Positively Powered Publications
Black Women in Business / Rose Smith and Deborah Cole. First edition.

ISBN 979-8-218-07196-7

This book is dedicated to all the women who have come before us,

those who are traveling with us and the ones who will come after us.

CONTENTS

Introduction
BY ROSE SMITH

"I had to make my own living and my own opportunity. But, I made it! Don't sit down and wait for the opportunities to come. Get up and make them."

—*Madam C. J. Walker*

SARAH BREEDLOVE—who later would become known as Madam C.J. Walker—is one of my biggest inspirations. She was an entrepreneur, activist and philanthropist. Madam C.J. Walker is recorded as the first female self-made millionaire in America, according to the *Guinness Book of World Records*. However, it was her mind and heart that intrigued my nine-year-old mind.

My maternal grandmother, Rosetta Ross, introduced me to the name of Madam C.J. Walker. As I squirmed and complained one Saturday morning while she attempted to "straighten" my hair, she mentioned the products and work of this extraordinary woman. And, even at nine years of age, I understood the level of success she had reached when my grandmother added she was the first woman to become a millionaire in the United States. When I began asking questions, she instructed me to visit the library to learn more about this amazing businesswoman.

As for hair straightening...

Black people have straightened their hair since the early 1900s, mainly due to discrimination. Although the process has been modernized, those old enough to remember after slavery was abolished, newly freed Black "Americans" were unprotected by the government. Jim Crow laws also made it difficult for them to take advantage of their rights as citizens and secure employment. To find a job and create a new life usually meant altering their hair texture in order to fit into European beauty standards.

Over the years, the more I read and learned about Madam C.J. Walker, her brilliant mind and entrepreneurial journey, the more she inspired me. Her desire to help women, uplift people and build the Black community was in direct alignment with my upbringing. Her confidence, courage and vision for herself and others was not only motivating, but very familiar. From what I discovered through reading, she reminded me of both my grandmothers, whom I was named after. Rosetta Ross (my maternal grandmother) and Rosie Chase (my paternal grandmother) were two of the most extraordinary women I have ever known. I share the life lessons that they taught me with others daily.

In a world where we often speak of generational curses, I am the product of generational blessings. I realize the sacrifices my ancestors made for me, and the only way I can show my gratitude is to pay it forward. We didn't have a perfect life. I don't think anyone does. It is what we make from the life we are born into that defines us.

INTRODUCTION

*"Train up a child in the way that he should go and
when he is old—he will not depart from it."*

—Proverbs 22:6

I was born into a life filled with love, faith, morals, hard work ethics, positive examples, a sense of family, love for community, self-worth, and respect for others. Despite my ancestors being forced into slavery, tormented by the KKK, picking cotton for pennies, attending segregated schools and being discriminated against all of their lives, they managed to not only hold on to but pass on the things that would help us all rise.

A strong positive mindset helps me get through difficult times. I believe that in the midst of chaos comes opportunity. So, I focus on what should be the priority and things I can do to make the current situation better. I use this mentality for everything and everyone. You would be surprised how your life will change if you have the same sense of urgency about helping others as you do about receiving help. Read that again.

In 2011, the vision to create the Black Women In Business (BWIB) platform was planted in my spirit. It caught me off guard, and honestly, I wasn't ready or willing to take on the challenge. Perhaps it stemmed from the fact that I lived in Austin, Texas, where Black people accounted for an estimated 7% of the population. In corporate America, it was the norm for some of us to go to work and not see another Black person until we returned home. This is a constant reminder that we are indeed the minority. The overall Austin population exploded between 2000 and 2010, growing over 20%. But a University of Texas study found that Austin was the only US city experiencing double-digit population growth that saw its Black population not only lose pace—but actually decline.

Some reasons for the decline are believed to be the gentrification of East Austin (now referred to as Central Austin by those who weren't born there, have never lived there prior to gentrification or lack generations of history tied to it). Over the years, gentrification has led to rising property values and taxes. It has forced black families to move or sell. Most have moved out of Austin into adjacent cities. So, only small traces of the "Negro District" established in 1928 remain.

As I stepped away from corporate life and into my entrepreneurial journey, I realized excuses previously mentioned were the best reasons for me to start the organization. Despite the fact that it took me three years to accept my calling, the birth of the organization was necessary. Black Women in Business would represent the underrepresented. The name itself insinuated strength and unity. It would promote success and sisterhood. And it would help change the narrative for Black-owned businesses.

At the inception of Black Women In Business in 2014, there were few Austin organizations with the word "Black" in their titles. "African American" was trending; somehow, it was perceived as politically correct and less offensive. At least, that is what I was told. Some of my Black "friends" and associates even questioned my choice and suggested I take a different route.

Fortunately, I have never been one to follow the crowd.

I stuck with Black. Why? My reason is simple. Nuance is important when discussing race in America or on a global scale. "Black" and "African American" are not always interchangeable. "African American" was typically used to refer to descendants of people from Africa who were enslaved. The term is nation specific. Some don't identify as African American because they cannot trace their lineage.

For me, Black isn't just about race—it's about culture. It is recognition of a larger community of people. It includes us all. Every person. Every journey. Every hardship. Every accomplishment. Every. Single. One of us.

The organization was designed to include business owners, those who aspire to own a business, corporate leaders, community advocates and women who needed a tribe of women to help them maximize their potential. This was a strategic choice. The mission of BWIB is to educate, encourage and empower businesswomen to excel in entrepreneurship and leadership. We are committed to enriching lives, families and communities by providing tools for personal growth, productivity and profit.

The organization is known as "A Movement" and is dedicated to a journey of self-confidence, sisterhood and success.

In the first year we attracted 125 members and for the next three consecutive years, membership ranged between 125 and 150 members, and excitement was in the air. The monthly meetings included icebreakers, business presentations, a motivational speaker, networking, fellowship and food. The meetings were enlightening and inspirational. We joked about there being a "meeting after the meeting," because most of us were so excited to be in each other's company that we would hang around laughing and talking, sometimes for hours after the real meeting had adjourned.

As a coach, I want women to become better from the inside out. I encourage them to do their inner work. It is super important for women to be confident in who they are in the present tense. So often, we want to wait to celebrate ourselves once we feel we are worthy. I need *you* to know you are worthy right now! The highs and lows of our lives have helped us become the incredible, resilient women we are today. I have watched shy women become outspoken leaders. I have worked to inspire partnerships and encourage collaborations. And over the years, I have had the pleasure of witnessing and experiencing friendships bloom between complete strangers. It is amazing what can happen when we believe in something greater than ourselves.

Between 2017 and the end of 2019, we launched nine additional chapters within the state of Texas. With Austin as our headquarters, we joyfully added San Antonio, Killeen, Dallas, San Marcos, Waco, Texas City, Fort Worth, Houston, and Manor. I traveled to each city for monthly meetings. Each chapter held monthly meetings, special events, networking mixers and served their communities as needed. As the founder, I want to be certain that our members understand the importance of serving others and giving back.

The organization houses a Scholarship Program, Teen Entrepreneurship Program and Community Food Relief Program. It provides these platforms so members have an opportunity to practice philanthropic activity. We host dozens of annual events, including Black Business Week, Community Easter Egg Hunt, Back to School Drive, and the Black Women In Business Extravaganza.

Our COVID Community Food Relief Program was created at the early stages of the pandemic. It was a time of uncertainty and fear for all of us. After asking God what He wanted me to do, I heard, "Serve the people." One evening I called two of my faithful BWIB members (Archette Royster and Briana Murphy) to share God's words in my vision to be obedient. Without a moment's hesitation, we were on a mission. I started the food relief program out of my very own pocket, and on March 16, 2020, we began delivering free groceries to seniors, residents with disabilities and families in need seven days a week.

In 2021, with the support and contributions of many amazing businesses, churches and individuals, this program grew into a *million* dollar program. Last year, WE THE PEOPLE invested more than a million dollars into Travis County families and individuals experiencing food disparities. The majority of the investment and work was invested in East Austin (District 1) families, which included more than a dozen multifamily complexes in the Eastern Crescent.

I will be forever grateful to my husband, Charles, our sons Debrico and Chandler, daughter Delissa, grandsons Daedrian and Micah and goddaughter, Jordan who joined me in the trenches as I worked to build an efficient program that could meet the needs of our community, capture data, manage pickups and deliveries, foster the relationships with our community partners and try to keep everyone safe. Your support means more than you know.

I would like to thank the Black Women in Business and community members who spearheaded our food relief program, including Briana Murphy, Jacqueline Freeman, Archette Royster, Cija Williams, Jocelyn Evans, Chris Asberry, Anye Smith, Deshay King, Katie Eichelberger, Jeannette Valdez Duran, Lavon Roe, Christopher Cutkelvin, Alexis Dean, Katii McKinney, Ro-Lunda Jackson, Tiara Moore-Jones, Haritha Haridass, Elder Ellis Branch, and the Street Liberators.

I want to thank our volunteers, the "BWIB Street Team," we couldn't do it without you. Thanks to Ballet Austin, Hoover's Cooking, Greater Mount Zion Church, Wheatsville Food Co-op, Tieks, Brawny, Live Oak Realty, Austin Christian Fellowship, Bethel Austin, Texas Banker's Foundation, Travis County Precinct 1 Constables, Deborah Cole Connections, Austin Starbucks, H.E.B, Glimmer Austin, Green Gate Farms, Austin Public Health, The Body Bar, Genell Sew Boutique, Educate 2 Empower, The Cook's Nook, Dia's

Market, The Street Liberators, African American Youth Harvest Foundation, Fund II Foundation, Black Leaders Collective, I Support the Girls, Eden East, Austin Area Urban League, Recognize Good, We Can Now, Revive U Restoration, Down South Cajun Eats, World Central Kitchen, The Flaming Pit, Dished By Kim LLC and Urban Power Connections, LLC.

The MVP Award goes to Austin Trader Joe's. They have donated high-quality food for the families we serve seven days a week for two years now. Not only do they donate so much food, but their employees and management come out to volunteer with us.

I must also thank individuals who believed in the vision and went above and beyond to assist. Commissioner Jeff Travillion, Constable Tonya Nixon, Pete Inman, Archbishop Sterling Lands, Greg and Lynne Dobson, Manor Council Member Emily Hill, Jeannette Valdez Duran and Ryan Coaxum.

The program is a true representation of people, businesses and organizations coming together to invest in the community. To date, we have delivered and served free groceries to more than 90,000 families with no governmental funding. The work has been hard, yet so many amazing women and men have shown up for more than two years to serve the community like family. As a society, we should understand that we all win when we invest in our youth, families in need, community and the next generation.

I am an advocate for women—all women. When women come together, great things happen. It doesn't matter the color of our skin, our economic background or our beliefs. Women are more likely to care for the collective, and more likely to step in when we see human suffering or injustice. Most women will invest their time in establishing practices and systems that "even the playing field" instead of widening the divide.

One woman alone has power, but together we have *impact*. Raising each other up and collaborating is how we change the game. We all want the same thing. We want to know we matter. We want to be heard and understood. We want to be supported and supportive. We want to be loved and celebrated. And, we want to have fun! But, most importantly, we want better—for ourselves, our families and the world we live in.

INTRODUCTION

"Resilience is very different than being numb. Resilience means you experience, you feel, you fail, you hurt. You fall. But you keep going."

—*Yasmin Mogahed*

Resilience is the ability to withstand adversity and bounce back from difficult life events. Being resilient doesn't mean we don't experience stress, loss, doubt ourselves, or at times want to quit. Resilience is the ability to continue on our journey even though we feel every one of those emotions. Some equate resilience with mental toughness, but demonstrating resilience includes working through emotional pain and suffering.

On the other side of resilience is strength, wisdom, compassion, understanding and gratefulness. It changes us at our core. There is no way to achieve resilience without going through something unpleasant. However, we do go through it.

Resilience is what you see when you look in the mirror. It is in the women in your family and in your circle. It is within every woman you will ever encounter.

We are honored to present to you *Black Women in Business: Journeys in Resilience.*

(All photos in this chapter are courtesy of Joi Conti Photography and Ivan Miller.)

SMITH

Black Women in Business

BLACK FEMALE ENTREPRENEURSHIP in Austin, Texas, would not be the expression of power that it is today without the vision and energy of Rose Smith, respectfully known as Coach Rose. She is the Founder and CEO of Black Women in Business, established in 2014 in Austin with a mission to unite, educate and inspire Black businesswomen to excel in leadership and entrepreneurship. Today, Coach Rose ensures that this mission is supported through coaching, compassion and community. Her intention is for the gifted and talented Black women of America to be welcomed and seen in business as well as the community.

The self-proclaimed "little country girl from Luling, Texas," felt a deep sense of kinship in her hometown as well as within her close-knit family. Rose's early years were spent as a part of a family that worked hard and achieved success in diverse occupations. Her maternal grandfather (Eugene Ross) was a World War II veteran, Exxon retiree (after thirty-five years) and a successful farmer. Rose's maternal grandmother

"My brand is love and inclusion."

(Rosetta Ross) was a domestic goddess and gardener, who was employed as the premier cook for an oil tycoon in their small hometown. Her paternal grandfather (Clem Chase) was a farmer and business owner, while her paternal grandmother (Rosie Chase) also made a name for herself as a domestic goddess, who loved music and fashion.

Thanks to her family, Rose developed talents in creative areas as well as growing up inspired by family members, who were industrious and committed to their vocations. She feels fortunate that the men in her family treated her as an equal. What was expected of the boys was expected of Rose. What they believed men could do, they also believed Rose could do. Her father was a motivating force in her life and would often say, "Rose, get out there and show them how to do it." Coach Rose hears stories of women treated differently than the young men in their families; however, she never experienced this. In school, as an athlete, cheerleader, band member or student she tackled and mastered every task and opportunity set in front of her. She credits her father with nurturing in her the belief that she was always capable. Rose learned to "make do" from her grandmother, who could make a lot from a little. She draws upon her family life lessons in her role leading a growing organization.

At nine, Rose experienced the traumatic loss of her beloved father (Clemmie Chase), who was her hero and one of her biggest inspirations today. It was he who told Rose, "You can do anything you put your mind to." She believed him.

The love and support of her maternal grandparents made it easy for Rose, her mother (Jean Chase) and three siblings to reside and thrive in their home. Rose was exposed to more life lessons taught by these loving relatives, and as an adult, Rose credits them with sharing not only their home but their

wisdom. The outgoing and precocious Rose feels she was uniquely different from her classmates and children her age. She observed people closely, asked a lot of questions and looked for ways to bring people together to accomplish more.

After the passing of her father, she was quickly introduced to the role of leadership as the oldest of her three siblings. She later became one of nine Black students in her high school graduating class. Whatever activity or interest she participated in, she always rose to a leadership position. She credits this to her mother and grandparents, who taught her commitment and discipline to every obligation, and she always brought her best to every responsibility.

Following high school graduation, Rose attended Wharton County Jr. College, then Blinn College, followed by later studies at the University of Texas at Austin. Her education lies in business and marketing, which were a perfect fit for her natural abilities to organize and manage "doing it all" in a people-centric manner. With a competitive spirit, confidence and lessons learned from her father, Rose engages a can-do attitude, trusting that whatever she (or anyone) desires can be accomplished with ample effort. Success for her is a love of what you want to do, doing the work to achieve it and then being satisfied with the results. Rose strongly believes that success is defined by each individual, not just how the world defines the term.

After relocating to Austin to attend the University of Texas, Rose found the mood of the community to be surprising and very different from any she had previously experienced. Segregation of races was evident in many parts of the city at that time, geographically and culturally. The atmosphere of "you're doing well for a Black girl" and similar less-than-supportive attitudes were a surprise to Rose, who had always felt supported before. The sense of cliquishness was new to her. However, it was also an opportunity to "change the game." She took the "vibe" as a challenge, using prickly situations as fuel for her fire to encourage inclusivity. She volunteered and plugged herself in to support change in such a separatist environment. Her hard work ethic, activist role and desire to help people win became her trademark. The success stories told by members of Black Women in Business are proof of the difference that Coach Rose and the organization have made in the community and in thousands of families' lives.

Her career path has been educational as well as productive. As a focused and industrious woman, Rose has been employed since the age of fourteen in a variety of jobs where she strategically used her talents, education and love for people to excel. In Austin, she quickly became a champion in marketing and sales with General Motors, MCI and other local communication companies. She used her talents of focus and tenacity to reinvent processes within the firms to encourage her employees and delight owners. Within each work environment, Rose has drawn upon her innate gifts and people skills. Although the work was satisfying, she found that opportunities to inspire and educate were even more rewarding. As a role model and Coach, she has always encouraged those in her orbit to use their own talents to be successful.

Rose has always sought to be helpful to others in the community but has had a special affinity for supporting Black women in their journeys. Having been a single mom for fourteen years, she understands the difficulties women experience "going it alone." With empathy for others, she shares lessons of strength and tenacity with the women she mentors, whether these involve personal or business challenges. As the sole role model for her biological son and daughter

(Debrico and Delissa Chase) until her marriage to the love of her life (Charles Smith), Rose was reminded by the wisdom of her maternal grandfather to sustain her strength in overcoming any adversities. With her husband, she shares the blessing of a blended family complete with six amazing children and nine beautiful grandchildren. She does not believe in using the word "step." She says that whenever we use the word step, it excludes someone. It places them on the outside of a relationship, and when it comes to children, could make them feel less loved. In her opinion, when it comes to family, it's hard to build when we separate.

In May of 2022, and during the birth of this book, Rose, aka "Coach," was presented with the 2022 I Am Austin Woman award. The Woman's Way Awards was created by *Austin Woman Magazine*. Their prerequisite for the award is as follows: "This woman is beloved in the Austin community for her innate ability to engage, empower and inspire those around her. Throughout her lengthy career and avid community involvement, she has led with exceptional grace and finesse, her actions echoing the core mission of Austin Woman Magazine. The impact she has made as a woman and for women is key." For Coach Rose, this was a full-circle moment. The young woman who had once moved to a city wondering where she would fit in was being recognized for standing out and standing up for Austin women. After decades of working in the Austin community, birthing two organizations (R.O.S.E.S—Reaching Out Supporting Every Sister, and Black Women in Business), serving her community, coaching thousands of women, employees, business owners and colleagues, and striving to inspire others by challenging herself—it is safe to say she understands what it takes to change the game.

"We *all* need encouragement," is one of Coach Rose's lessons. She advises that in order to become a better businesswoman, you must become a better woman first. Along with business expertise, Rose reminds everyone to consider their encounters with others an opportunity to improve their lives. She has always sought to find ways to help others, to improve their situation, to make them smile and to leave them in a better place than when she met them. She shares these lessons with others and encourages them to incorporate servicing others in their business lives. Being willing to help and encouragement are keys to success in business and in living a happy life. "We don't become powerful by what we do. We become powerful by what we inspire others to do," she says. Coach Rose is the embodiment of love, encouragement and inclusion.

"Don't ask what the world needs. Ask what
makes you come alive, and go do it.

Because what the world needs is
people who have come alive."

~Howard Thurman

Sophia
STEWART ADAMS

SO SO GOOD COOKING LLC

SOPHIA STEWART ADAMS has always been a woman of creativity, responsibility and hard work. On any given day, you may find her wielding her tools of the trade as a chef in her steamy kitchen, prepping for a catered meal for dozens or dreaming up new blends of spices for her popular line of seasonings.

As the oldest girl in a household of six children in Anchorage, Alaska, she was often tasked with "looking after things." Even though she had two older brothers, her parents knew that Sophia was the reliable one and could take charge whenever called upon. As a conscientious caregiver, Sophia excelled at the challenge and even discovered an early love for cooking and food preparation.

Not a fan of cold and dark Alaskan winters, Sophia left home after high school graduation and moved to Texas, where she attended the University of Texas at Arlington. She graduated with a major in social work but learned during her internship

"Just let my ego go!"

that the realities of working closely with clients affected by dementia would not be the vocational path she wanted to follow. In any mental health profession, practitioners find it necessary to maintain complete emotional distance from their clients in order to be most effective. Sophia found she became closely attached to her assigned patients, which prevented her from maintaining objectivity.

As she considered a shift in career, Sophia looked to what was tugging at her heart. She knew that her love language was food preparation and service and that creativity and the execution of meals were her passions. She first experimented with her recipes, cooking for family and friends on a trial basis using her own unique blends of seasonings and spices. These first "customers" always asked how she flavored her distinctive dishes and wanted to know how she blended the seasonings. The common request from her friends and family was, "We want to buy these!" When she offered to prepare the dishes for them, her catering business was launched.

At first, she cooked for casual occasions such as baby showers and birthday parties. Family and friends referred others to her and as she was asked to cook for larger events, her business began to grow. A close friend advised her on the details of the business side of operations. Sophia listened carefully to all the advice for So So Good Cooking LLC and learned the steps to obtaining necessary permits and licenses before she launched a website, in order to have everything operating as a proper, legal entity. She also developed cooking demonstrations which she posted to a growing Instagram account, which currently boasts almost 22,000 followers.

The catering business was growing quickly just as the global pandemic arrived in 2019 and early 2020. Although this ended her rapid growth and catering

ground to a halt, Sophia was not concerned. The "pause" gave her the opportunity to focus on further experimentation with her line of seasonings, the essential components of many of her dishes. She officially launched her seasoning line in 2020, and even though her catering business was on hold, she was able to vigorously promote the new line.

Over the course of several months, Sophia perfected seven seasoning blends for meats, veggies, seafood and tacos, plus an additional mixture for seafood fry and a barbecue rub. She made these available through her website and Instagram, which remain her primary online sales platforms.

In the Dallas-Fort Worth area, she has been featured in publications such as *VoyageDallas* and *Shoutout DFW* magazines, which helped to boost sales of her seasonings. Both interviews and features resulted from Sophia's consistent messaging through Instagram. Her most recent interview with *CanvasRebel Magazine* (also sourced through Instagram) has added to the notoriety Sophia has developed in the Metroplex.

As the pandemic restrictions eased, Sophia reestablished her catering services. She sells seasonings and provides "pop-up catering" in temporary festival venues. One of her newest offerings is her series of self-sponsored pop-up dinners with food provided by So So Good Catering. She provides a five-course meal with music and an open bar, and each patron leaves with samples of the seasonings used in the meal.

Lessons in resilience appear in different forms, whether external or personal. Both in our personal as well as business lives, we meet obstacles that are outside of our control. Situations arise, and we respond. We either succumb or dig deep to survive and thrive. As a young girl, Sophia developed independence and self-sufficiency, which gave her the strength to strike out on her own and leave her hometown in Alaska. These qualities gave her the strength to make a change in professions when she realized that her degree would not serve her as a satisfying profession. And she possessed the strength to strike out on her own to start a business following where her heart led. The same independence that nudged Sophia to do new and great things also borders on being headstrong. In retrospect, the belief that she must do everything herself and not ask for help might have hindered her progress. She has learned to let go of control in order not to burn out early in the game of building a business. Changing patterns of behavior creates strength and is the true badge of a resilient leader. Sophia believes that the advice and support through Black Women in Business only adds to the education of all its members.

It is only natural to feel that abrupt changes in business plans are a negative; however, the slowdown in catering propelled Sophia's development of new seasoning mixes and motivated her to participate in festivals, whether cooking or selling those seasonings. Having successfully navigated some regional festivals, she has her sights on participating in the Essence Festival in New Orleans, where over 500,000 people attend each year. Another target is the three-week Texas State Fair in Dallas, Texas, where over two million attend each year.

As Sophia advises, it is important to stay focused on personal passion and goals. She emphasizes the need to stay the course and not be lured into producing other products or services which are not a part of the plan. Learning to say "no" is important. However, if opportunities present themselves for furthering the vision, reply with a strong "yes" and work hard to make it happen. Sophia is proof that this philosophy is a true "yes."

Tanisha

BARNETT

NATURE'S HIDDEN TREASURES

TANISHA BARNETT is a native of Austin, who believes that women have no limits. Being a wife and mother of two has never limited her in fulfilling her personal or professional dreams. She advocates for all women who have ambitions and encourages all to imagine the best for themselves while they "dream big."

Reports indicate that over half of the world's female population give up on their dreams and feel dissatisfied with their professional lives. Achieving dreams often means many sacrifices must be made. This effort requires skills, incredible energy, resources and support. Even though the same is true for men, they don't stop dreaming at the same rate as women. Advisors suggest to women that they be sensible, be realistic and take the safe route. Because of such flawed advice, women tend to give up and often appear less imaginative or ambitious. Tanisha is helping women to overcome such notions.

"Be yourself."

As an adolescent, Tanisha saw herself growing into a life as a corporate executive, living in a large city in a high-rise, single and with no children. In real life, she married her high school sweetheart and has two young daughters, which she believes is the different calling that God intended for her. When her little ones showed signs of skin and hair problems, she researched and sought solutions. All of the commercial remedies she found on the market failed to produce positive results, and she formulated her own products. Using natural ingredients, she produced formulations which resulted in improvements for her entire family, including her husband. She shared her preparations with other family members and friends, who found the same positive results. When Tanisha was encouraged to manufacture and sell her formulations commercially, she began to consider the possibility of starting her own business. She had previously worked in pharmaceuticals until she made the decision to focus on her family, and the fit was a natural one.

One of the first phone calls Tanisha made as her business plan took shape was to Black Women in Business in Austin. Her first question was the same that many newly minted entrepreneurs have, "Where do I start?" She had the vision and passion but was lacking in the nuts and bolts of business savvy. The answer: ensure that the brand was an accurate and true representation of Tanisha and her values.

The business grew much more quickly than Tanisha imagined, initially through word of mouth and later through her website and social media. She knew that a website was essential for business success. A web presence plus social media help to reach potential customers, allow shoppers to buy 24/7, create credibility by providing education and information and notify potential buyers of events and current happenings within the business.

Although social media is a necessity for business promotion, a combination of all the platforms plus a website has proven to give the best results. Social media is good for generating leads, and the website channels lead to sales. Tanisha is an advocate for all forms of lead generation and sales. She maintains a website and a Facebook account, as well as active Instagram postings, where she shares news, upcoming events and products.

While the primary inspiration for creating a natural skin and hair care line was to address family health concerns, a secondary motivation for building a company was to provide a model of entrepreneurship for her girls. Tanisha's drive to build generational wealth is important to demonstrate to her children as well. She has a kids' line called NHT Gems Kids Collection, inspired by her daughters. It provides them the opportunity to have input into the business and know that they are a part of the creative as well as the operational side of the company. The line was launched in 2022 at Youthpreneur, a women's history month event. All three Barnetts participated.

Tanisha believes that while growing up, she was "in training" for her role as a future entrepreneur. She was involved in extracurricular activities where she learned networking, communication and leadership, and participated in scholarship pageants where she honed her skills in ambassadorship and branding. Her activities now, whether business or personal, are mirror images of her extracurricular activities as a teen. The skill sets she learned and mastered early are exactly what sets her apart as a business owner in today's marketplace.

When things got hard or business slowed, Tanisha credits her customers with providing her the motivation to achieve. She heard accounts of how much her customers not only loved her products but what a difference they had made for them. These reports were enough to encourage her to continue growing her business. The customers were the fuel to her fire of resilience.

The balance of work and personal life is important to Tanisha and was never more so than during 2020–2021. She feels that she can give 110% to everything she does; however, when she feels the need to take a hard pause to give herself space for reflection, she does that without hesitation. The death of two family members caused her to take much-needed personal time before recommitting fully to her business. Recognizing the need for self-care is a part of the journey from stress to wellness and is true resilience in action.

Tanisha is active in the community in addition to her role as an entrepreneur. She is the founder of the Miss Juneteenth Texas pageant, a program that provides mentorship, promotes youth empowerment and teaches the history and culture of the Black community as well as the importance of community service. The vision and mission of the program is to encourage young women to have self-confidence and high self-esteem. Tanisha has also been a speaker at local small business events in central Texas and has been named one of the 250 Most Influential African Americans in Central Texas.

As author Stephen Covey writes, "Most people spend their whole lives climbing the ladder of success only to realize, when they get to the top, the ladder has been leaning against the wrong wall," and they give up. Providing natural products which change people's lives through improved health was Tanisha's purpose. Her ladder was definitely leaning against the right wall.

Dr. Kerri CARTER-WALKER

DR. KERRIE

LIKE THE MAJORITY OF THE MEMBERS of Black Women in Business, Dr. Kerrie Carter-Walker is a multi-talented, multifaceted woman. "Multi" seems to be an aptly descriptive term for every aspect of her life. On the flip side, her brand is simple. Those who know her know that her near-iconic brand name—Dr. Kerrie—says so much. She is a business owner, a successful realtor, a role model and mentor for young women who benefit from her life lessons and wisdom. Her purpose is to help young women to discover and love who they are authentically. She encourages doing this with intentional dialogue in order to uncover their true purpose in life.

Dr. Kerrie was born in the small town of Cuero, Texas. Although outsiders may have believed her family life to be without difficulty, Dr. Kerrie experienced the childhood trauma of abuse and unsupported parental homelife, which would affect her mental health and relationships well into adulthood.

"You have everything in you."

She attended Concordia College, graduating with a bachelor's degree in kinesiology. While at Concordia she played on the basketball team until she tore her anterior cruciate ligament (ACL) and could no longer play. Fortunately, she was allowed another year of eligibility and went on to earn her master's degree in Curriculum and Instruction.

After completing her graduate work, she was hired as an assistant principal at then Reagan High School in Austin. (The school has been renamed and is now known as Northeast Early College High School.) While working as assistant principal, Dr. Kerrie began her PhD work at Concordia-Portland, completing this degree in 2020. After a year at Reagan, Dr. Kerrie was relocated to LBJ High School and then Akins High School for what turned out to be her final assignment as assistant principal. An abrupt, unexpected separation from her position resulted in severe emotional distress, and she realized she needed to become anchored in her faith.

At the time of her resignation from her position with the Austin Independent School District, Dr. Kerrie realized she had two choices. She could continue to experience anxiety and take no action to rediscover what she knew to be her authentic self, or she could begin the difficult work of healing that would lead to a more satisfying life of peace and joy.

During the time she was an assistant principal, she listened to her friends talk about businesses they had started. The businesses might be considered side hustles; however, she listened carefully and knew that she was also capable and motivated to do the same.

Today her professional life is exactly what and where she wants it to be. The transformation was not easy, however, and often frightening. Dr. Kerry credits

her faith in God as the power that helped her heal her early traumas and to draw on her own strength in order to make necessary life changes. As she was pulled into dark places following her exit from the educational field, she believed in a higher power and in herself to make those changes—necessary for her own good and the good of those she was called on to help.

Dr. Kerrie has found her passion and calling in the form of businesswoman, coach and speaker. She has drawn on her life experiences to enrich each part of her professional life. As a real estate investor who subsequently obtained her real estate license, Dr. Kerrie also represents New Hope Realty Group. In this capacity, she listens to the needs and dreams of home buyers. As an empathetic partner in their search for a special residence, she advises potential homeowners and helps them to find the perfect solution. Her natural talents and skills as an educator make her an ideal match for those looking to buy a home.

As the founder of the business iSquared Coaching, Dr. Kerrie has developed a program for young women aged twelve to eighteen that addresses self-esteem issues, conflict resolution, time management and other topics that are not part of a public-school curriculum. Dr. Kerrie offers this program to seventy-five students in Austin Independent School Districts in order to fill in gaps missing from young girls' lives. Girls need to hear the message of empowerment.

Dr. Kerrie is an enthusiastic member of Black Women in Business. After experiencing the power of the collective group of women, she believed that this organization was a good place for her. And although she spoke to groups large and small in her capacity as an educator, she had never thought of herself as a motivational speaker. When CEO Rose Smith asked her to create a presentation for an annual Conference and Extravaganza, Dr. Kerrie was quick to accept. She had felt that her personal message and lessons learned through trauma and healing might resonate with groups, and she was delighted at the positive feedback she received after her first presentation. Her public speaking career was launched.

Recently, Dr. Kerrie created a podcast called "More Than The Bag." She uses this medium to point to alternatives to "chasing the wrong bag." Young women often focus on fields of study, careers and personal life decisions that are not in their best interest. In her own life, until she awakened to the need for her own self-reflection and healing, she was chasing the wrong bag. The weight of childhood trauma can cause poor decision-making. Dr. Kerrie encourages ideas and ways to break the cycle of trauma as well as generational curses. Through her podcast, other social media and YouTube videos, her coaching emphasizes faith in oneself. Her message is that although our childhood created us, we have choices to make later in life.

Dr. Kerrie credits prayer, meditation and affirmations with helping her heal the psychological injuries of childhood. When she chose to change her life because it was not the life she wanted, she was able to apply what she learned through these practices to her life and her teaching. Through coaching and listening, she shares many of her successful techniques with others.

Firm in her faith, when at a crossroads moment, when she had the decision to give up or move forward in her life, she listened to God. He told her that He had more to do through her. And she chose God. Dr. Kerrie firmly believes in her power and in her abundance. And she believes in the ability of women to achieve whatever they desire. She is a model of faith, courage and resilience.

212 CATALYSTS

IT IS DIFFICULT TO CHOOSE the best word that describes the impressive energy of BiNi. Is her descriptor "catalyst" or is it "action"? Most would say it's a powerful combination of both.

As founder and CEO of 212 Catalysts, BiNi supports various agencies, both large and small, in their mission-critical business operations. Her goal is to ensure that, through collaborative community involvement, their development goals are met. She had a critical role in the launch of the African American Leadership Institute and worked to establish or improve systems for the Austin Independent School District, Texas Muslim Women's Foundation, People's Community Clinic and African American Youth Harvest Foundation.

The name of her company illustrates the power of making a difference. The boiling point of water is 212 degrees Fahrenheit. It is at this point that a change in the state of being of water occurs. One degree less and nothing changes. One extra degree

"Catalyzing action that leads to results."

makes a difference. As BiNi says, "the margin for good to great is small." Her video tells the story of how small changes can be made by individuals to make a difference in the world (see the Resources/References). Small differences do matter.

As a child growing up in a beautifully blended family in Garland, Texas, BiNi cannot remember a day when race was not a topic of conversation in her household. As a biracial girl, her parents encouraged extensive discussions about race. BiNi not only experienced a childhood of rich conversations, but she also grew up in a family of compassion and deep concern for causes where people mattered. She felt that whether the German heritage of her mother was the cause for strength of conviction, or it was the simple "hardheadedness" that bonded her to serving others, either way her family knew what to do to lift others up. As she grew up, she sought ways to serve others. This innate drive to help, coupled with creative traits, has propelled her to professional success.

As a student at the University of Texas, BiNi was a member of the volleyball team as well as the recipient of an academic scholarship. During the first summer, she serendipitously found employment at a summer camp called Kids Across America. Although, at the time, her intention was to work in the corporate arena in a large metropolitan area, the camp and the kids "grew on her." She found that she had a gift for working with kids, who likewise gravitated to her. This natural ability to bring individuals together to work as a cohesive unit evolved from eight summers at Kids Across America to her eventual professional life. Ultimately, she realized she wanted to not only make a difference in the business world, but to make a difference in the lives of those in her community.

While working in the world of business administration and finance, BiNi could only dream of a day when she would be able to do work benefiting

the community and making a living doing it. A recruiter for the Austin Independent School District happened to notice BiNi had experience working with youth in a resume on file, and rather than place her in a finance position, for which she had applied, she was asked to lead a program in the Community Education department. AISD had federal grant funding for a leadership position with the 21st Century Community Learning Center as a part of the campus improvement strategy. A site coordinator had left, leaving the program adrift. The challenge would be to rebuild the program after the departure of the coordinator. BiNi started working in this administrative side with one school, then oversaw several.

Taking the school and students in the program from a place of bad morale and low esteem, BiNi improved the program not only in the initial target school, but subsequently in ten schools. Under BiNi's leadership, the after-school programs for older students were nationally recognized for their academic outcomes. Following the successes within the Austin Independent School District, she began her consulting practice with agencies such as the Texas Education Agency, working with a statewide team of grantees to ensure their success in comparable programs.

BiNi continued to consult until she was recruited again by Austin Independent School District to assist with coordinating partnerships with various nonprofits. After completing successful foundational programs with AISD, she again felt the calling to broaden her focus of helping a broader community by creating 212 Catalysts.

212 Catalysts was formed in 2019 as a nonprofit, in order to work within multiple systems. BiNi has learned that often organizations are able to work

best with 501(C)3 individuals and groups as they navigate grants, improvements and changes. Her consulting business has continued to grow and now serves many types of businesses as well as educational organizations.

As BiNi gained experience and real-world wisdom (along with earning her MBA) she now specializes in community improvement through conversation and collaboration. Strategic planning, fundraising support, training and technical assistance are all a part of BiNi's consulting practice. She also provides key knowledge and training for operational issues, finance and project management. By helping agencies and diverse industries, she is "right in the middle" of improving community.

Connecting the dots to provide advice and support for improving the lives of those in her community is BiNi's consulting sweet spot. She loves working with broad-based groups on how to achieve results through diversification and collaboration. She works with agencies and organizations to assist in processes and include the right teams, even walking alongside as they implement. The results and outcomes are "magical."

BiNi's work seems to never be complete. Her mentoring and speaking engagements locally and nationally continue to provide education and support for students and leaders alike. As an active member of Black Women in Business, she offers support for others who are in the development mode of their businesses. She has served on over thirty boards, councils and networks throughout the country, and she has been recognized by local and national organizations for her community leadership and activism. BiNi is on a mission to serve and support, with the community as the beneficiary of her boundless energy. She is a catalyst in her own right.

Sianni DEAN

CRANKY GRANNY'S SWEET ROLLS

MANY ARTICLES ARE WRITTEN by and about young entrepreneurs and how they started their successful businesses. Few of these articles specifically focus on female entrepreneurs and even fewer on teenage business founders. Often these resourceful young women are written off as hobbyists and less-than-serious real business-people. Sixty-two percent of all women business owners are between the ages of forty and fifty-nine. Around 80% of these women have college degrees, statistics show. Supposedly, building and gathering experience takes a lot of time, which explains why only 30% of these women are younger than forty. Yet this "truth" is simply not true in all cases. Austin now claims as one of its own a brilliant and driven young woman who began a successful business at sixteen while in high school.

Sianni Dean is the founder and owner of Cranky Granny's Sweet Rolls, a booming business located in Austin. The business not only delivers some of the best and most flavorful

"I'm going to turn this negative energy into something positive."

sweet rolls ever, but it also has the mission of connecting people with one another through amazing confections filled with love.

Sianni's story begins in Willingboro Township, New Jersey, where she was an enthusiastic participant in an entrepreneurship class in high school. In the class, the students gained valuable information from lessons focused on starting, running and growing a business. She also listened to her dad, who informally taught her practical lessons about supply and demand as well as other real-life, everyday lessons of business. Although she entered yearly class competitions where she presented new and innovative business enterprise ideas to seek funding, she was not a winner. This did not deter her. She believes she had two choices—succeed OR succeed. Failure in her goals was not an option.

At the same time she was learning entrepreneurial skills, she also recognized her love for baking. As a high school freshman, she attempted enrollment in a baking and pastry class where only upperclassmen were accepted. When the teacher refused to admit Sianni, she pivoted and signed up for the same teacher's extracurricular baking club. After being admitted to the class officially, Sianni pooled her love of baking with her keen interest in building a business. The new baking and catering venture was fueled by a slightly broken heart. With lots of support, her early customers were mainly family and friends, and these were followed by an extensive customer base. Baked goods, food platters and catering services kept Sianni busy and financially independent as a teenager. She credits market research done between the ages of fifteen and eighteen and her entrepreneurial spirit with her early successes.

The claim that it takes years of dedication, commitment, and hard work to succeed in building connections, relationships, and capital to run a business

effectively is simply not true. Statistically, most women-owned companies are started when their founders were between the ages of forty and fifty-nine; however, Sianni is an excellent example of how someone decades younger can achieve business success through drive, research and hard work.

As a sixteen-year-old, the relationship breakup was a part of the motivation for the original launch of her business. At nineteen, a rift between Sianni and her mother fueled her decision to move from New Jersey to Texas, where she would sell her baked goods in a friend's restaurant. Although she considered this a risky move, she knew that failure was not an option. She had created a large following in her hometown in New Jersey, and she felt confident she could do it again.

After a brief visit to investigate Austin, and its possibilities, she made her move in the spring of 2020. Within four months, Sianni had rebuilt a robust customer base while promoting and selling her sweet rolls through the friend's restaurant. She then signed a lease for her first brick-and-mortar space.

The business, Cranky Granny's Sweet Rolls, which began as an idea in a high school setting, was headed for success. Working with her baking and pastry teacher/mentor in high school, she had already tested and tasted different doughs and flavors. As part of market research, Sianni ran surveys and trials of several names with family and friends. Calling on her entrepreneurial talents, Sianni crafted the name Cranky Granny's, which pays homage to her grandmothers and conjures up images of anyone's own grandma and their feisty personalities. Austin became home to the newest trending sweet treat with its diverse flavors, names and creative looks.

Sianni considers herself resilient during various times of her early business years. She believes baking and marketing the products were an antidote to a broken heart. Turning a negative around is her nature and also that of many successful entrepreneurs. With her business on an upward trajectory, she felt she needed to leave home and relocate to start afresh. Sianni looked for ways to retool and restart her business in a new location, finding incredible results through social media.

Every entrepreneur can learn from generations younger than themselves. These include the value of social media in business building. Consistent and well-targeted social media posts yield results. Sianni currently has over 44,000 followers on her Instagram account and finds amazing success with Facebook and TikTok videos featuring new offerings (bacon, egg and ham sweet rolls or fried chicken sweet rolls). The power of social media has propelled her into the upper limits of success in Austin since arriving in 2021. Sianni and Cranky Granny's Sweet Rolls have been featured in various publications, including Forbes, but it is the power of social media that has boosted her sales; that and the most delicious offerings (20 different flavors) imaginable.

Sianni is an independent, proud and focused woman who believes it important for her to be recognized as a talented, creative and motivated entrepreneur. Firm in her belief that she does not want to receive special favors or misdirected special consideration, she is a proud black, gay and young female entrepreneur. Although Sianni has found that her age has caused more challenges in being taken seriously than any other of her identities, she knows that it isn't an impediment to her success. Sianni is an entrepreneur. Know her for that.

Sonya
HOWARD

ActionCOACH Business Coaching

SONYA HOWARD IS AN ATLANTA NATIVE

Black Women in Business member living outside of the state of Texas. When CEO Rose Smith expanded membership to include women other than Texas residents, Sonya was ready and eager to join.

After graduating from high school, Sonya joined the U.S. Navy and was trained as an airplane mechanic. After her separation from the navy, she attended Georgia State University, graduating with a degree in Computer Information Systems. She then worked for numerous companies in Quality Assurance for twenty-three years advancing through the ranks until, as a manager, she was certified as a coach. In this role, Sonya trained and supported executives and directors in IT for the last ten years of her employment.

As a seasoned mentor, Sonya seized an opportunity to become an independent coach in her own business, which is what she does today. She utilizes all of the skills she obtained

"I walk alongside my clients."

during her time coaching executives under the umbrella of a coaching franchise to support others in achieving personal and business goals. Although the franchise industry is best known for restaurants, there are countless other services which are supported through the franchise structure. Over eight million people in the United States are employed by franchise businesses. Every one in seven businesses is a franchise. Franchises have a higher success rate than startup businesses. One of the bonuses for business owners who have a franchise is that there is a 90% success for franchises versus 15% for independently started businesses.

Although Sonya will never decline anyone who needs help, her primary focus is the support of Black women in every stage of their business cycle. She consults with women in the earliest stage of their businesses, many of whom launched in 2020 and 2021. She also works with clients who have been in business for several years and is comfortable working with entrepreneurs at any stage of their business life.

Many of the lessons in her coaching curriculum are ones that she targets for herself. She believes it is always important to sharpen one's own saw before teaching others to do the same. Initially, she works with goal setting and purpose definitions. Targets are key to being successful. Sonya and the client work together as a team on objectives and strategies. She then works on a marketing and sales' plan. In a questioning session, she asks about sales and revenue goals to start the conversation about realistic and attainable targets. Some of Sonya's advice includes analysis of the number of leads, the conversion rate, returning business and how much is spent. Lastly, the desired profits are also part of the conversation. As Sonya says, all advisors and coaches must be focused on numbers and metrics. Conversations between mentors and mentees must

be numbers driven. Accountability for success in reaching the numbers is an ongoing topic for discussion.

As a marketing maven, Sonya is also a marketing role model for her clients and always seeks out leads in order to locate individuals she can help/coach in their businesses. She is involved in business-to-business lead generation, virtual networking, social media, connection through LinkedIn and many other strategies, using over 300 ways to connect with potential clients. Whether virtually, on the phone or in person, she connects with those whose businesses she can help to meet their goals. Defining the purpose and setting goals, if they have none, is priority number one.

One of the benefits of connecting with Sonya for coaching is an initial no-obligation discovery meeting. After listening to their needs and desires, she asks potential clients questions about their business plans. Sonya assists in the development of a set of strategies for them to take their business to a higher level. If they decide to engage her coaching services, an extensive game plan is made. With or without further coaching, the client is armed with some new tactics for business growth and improvement.

For Sonya, coaching is all about education and walking alongside her clients as they build their businesses. She helps them think outside of the box. Her role is to encourage them to consider the business side of the organization they lead, not just the operational side of it. Once she has them considering the business of doing business, she helps with strategies so they can achieve the goals they have set.

Most important in any strategy is accountability. Coach Sonya meets with her clients weekly to provide support and ensure they are acting on their business "homework." The relationship is a partnership to advance both the business and the owner.

Prior to becoming a professional business coach, Sonya recognized her desire to be a listening partner for others in her personal life. As she approached using this gift with intention, she recognized that while her desire to help was not best used in a one-to-one situation; she was attracted to helping with groups. She helped form a specialized Girl Scout troop in the Arrendale State Prison, focusing on girls whose moms were incarcerated. Scouts and their moms participated in this nontraditional group with Sonya as the leader. She understood that 80% of girls whose moms are or have been in prison often suffer future family traumas and may eventually serve time themselves. The troop was formed with the goal of ending this cycle. Moms and daughters engaged in frank conversations led by Sonya, who first shared her story of her own teenage trauma—a trauma which followed her for twenty years. By sharing her own personal story, she was able to dramatically impact these young girls. By going deep and becoming vulnerable, she found that the young girls also had the courage to go deep and become vulnerable in telling their stories.

Sonya also visited young girls in group homes to share some of the same stories and communicate similar lessons. Her message was one of hope and promise, because she had experienced many of the same difficulties that they had. She shared stories of being "a hot mess" as a teen, but "look where I am now," crediting her faith in God and paying attention to where she was led. Her promise of "you can be whatever you want to be" is powerful.

Through Facebook Live, she brings messages of vulnerability, hope, grace and promise. Her message of courage and faith as a woman helps others to gain strength in their times of difficulties. Sonya's ability to relate to women and her desire to help them know better ways is directly based upon her own teenage trauma. Her ability to empathize and be a support system for those in need is a thread running through her life and into her coaching business. Whether counseling young women on personal issues or diving into intense business topics, Sonya's goal is to walk alongside each person as they gain a solid footing on the path toward success.

Kela (Chef Keii) HUNTE

KEII BRANDS, INC.

OCCASIONALLY, YOU MEET PEOPLE who seem otherworldly. At a young age, they exhibit creativity, wisdom and a sense of knowing that far exceeds their age. Born Kela Hunte, Chef Keii is a larger-than-life chef, baker and all-around amazing woman who has overcome an early life of adversity. She is full of knowledge, curiosity and fun, just the person you enjoy being in a room with. But the incredible, energetic personality is only a small part of a driven woman who advises that each business has a life of its own and hasn't asked to be birthed. The feeling of responsibility to this living entity is major and not to be taken lightly. Her joy and humor are close companions to a focused entrepreneurial commitment.

Life wasn't always so cheerful for Chef Keii. She grew up in a racist beach community in Florida, the daughter of a Barbadian (Bajan) father and American mother. Growing up as the child of parents who made poor life choices and lost custody of their children, Chef Keii relied on her innate

"My contribution to the world defines me, not my looks."

47

abilities to learn quickly, absorb information and be curious about the world. This was her source of stability. She dove into the world of books, where she found comfort as well as knowledge. An intuitive learner, Chef Keii appreciates her hunger for knowledge and credits it with being a stabilizing influence on her. At a young age, she knew that in order to have stability and the life she wanted, self-reliance was essential. The life that she was living was not the life she wanted to experience as an adult. Her self-acknowledged resilience is derived from a deep source which connects her with the energy of people around her. Chef Keii can observe and very quickly "read" a person. As a child, this ability was confusing for her; however, as an adult being able to read the energy and body language of those she meets is an advantage.

Chef Keii is a self-sufficient and confident woman and has worked hard to achieve success in what might be considered a male-dominated profession. As an assertive, not aggressive, woman, she is confident and proud of her accomplishments. Being a champion for change in a profession dominated by men is important to her.

In 2012, Chef Keii left a full-time job to become the caregiver for her son, who had sustained a life-threatening accident. Without a steady income, she sought ways to support her family. She started baking as a way to relieve stress during this rough period. Her first batch of cookies was disappointing. The perfectionist in her demanded her to do better. Hours of research on YouTube, Pinterest and reading cookbooks led her to a full life of perfecting and baking. Since she didn't allow her children to have sugar, she gave away everything she baked. Soon she received orders and "baked her way out of poverty." It still had not occurred to her to build a business from her baking. Throughout her son's rehabilitation, she continued to bake to provide family

support until Hurricane Irma caused her to relocate to Texas. Multiple services in central Texas provided her with housing, startup funds and the opportunity to receive training in a new career at the Auguste Escoffier School of Culinary Arts, where she double majored in culinary and pastry arts.

Once she arrived at culinary school, she found herself and "her people." She knew she was exactly where she needed to be. During this time, Chef Keii juggled a job, school and numerous volunteering gigs. She was determined to make the most of this opportunity to live her passion. In 2020, after Chef Keii had completed her education at culinary school, The Food Network reached out to the school and asked who they might recommend for an upcoming series starring Martha Stewart for a competitive cooking show featuring America's six top home bakers, and she was chosen. With the notoriety received from being on a national television program, Chef Keii began to receive requests to teach cooking classes. Apple, eBay, PayPal and event planners contacted her to create food events where she brought her natural teaching skills and personality to the work environment. The hobby which lifted her out of poverty was now an established business.

The business was officially born during the early days of 2020. Using her creativity, Chef Keii developed a "classes-in-a-box" concept, where she purchased and shipped ingredients directly to her students, as well as producing instructional videos where she demonstrated how to make each dish. Perhaps the first to do this, her classes-in-a-box became super popular, so popular that she reduced the time spent baking and focused on teaching. Through her business partnership with the international company PayPal, she has shipped kits around the world and has taught over 3,500 students how to prepare a variety of dishes as a part of the corporate team-building initiative.

Through her various business entities, she continues to teach virtually, to bake and to create special culinary events. Most recently, she developed a five-course workshop called "Recipes of Freedom" for Black History Month. She is also the founder of Chefs United Through Service, whose mission is to elevate participants' self-confidence and enhance mindfulness by using food as a canvas. Her current business model includes "ghost baking" services for a multitude of local restaurants. She's also developing new recipes and creating a unique, new candy bar.

She has launched a corporate umbrella, Keii Brands, Inc., which is a parent company for Keii Desserts, Keii Brands Entertainment, Keii Brands Apparel and the nonprofit Chefs United Through Services. The mission of the brands is to provide custom food experiences and related products.

The personality and the energy of this resilient single mother who has moved beyond a childhood of trauma fuels every action she takes. Although, by all accounts, she is at the top of her game, riding high on the successes of culinary school followed by media fame, she believes she still has room to grow and to learn. Chef Keii believes that success is not only personal but is also a reflection of how you can impact others in the community and in the world. As a model of integrity, standards and quality, she inspires others. Her advice for others is "if you aren't self-disciplined, not willing to learn, and not willing to be of service, do not start a business." Chef Keii believes she has an obligation as a Black woman to represent entrepreneurs who are resilient and overcome adversity. She wants everyone to know, "This is what progress looks like." Although she doesn't believe she has fully arrived, everyone who has met her believes she is on her way. She is a role model of success and resilience.

Kimberly (Kimber) McCarver

LeNoire Sugar

WOMEN, WHEN ASKED how they balance relationships, family, career, continuing education, community involvement, an emerging business and self-care, the answer is often, "with difficulty." Kimber McCarver, a native Austinite, has all of these activities on a daily "to-do" list that would exhaust most individuals. But with ease and grace and the resilience of a pro, she makes it look easy.

Kimber has been a member of the Apple, Inc. team for over five years while raising two children with her husband. Within only a few hours of completing her degree in business administration at Huston-Tillotson University, she became the co-founder of Noir Creators Space. This market in Pflugerville, Texas, is also known as the "Black farmers market" and is one of the first vendor spaces created within the city that provides BIPOC (Black, Indigenous, (and) People of Color) business owners a venue to showcase their products and services. In addition, as a volunteer and activist, Kimberly generously shares her time and energies with the

> *"You're not going to believe how good your life will be."*

community. Her solution to getting all of this accomplished? Paying attention to balance and faith, with a hefty dose of strength.

In 2016, the loss of Kimber's grandmother coincided with postpartum depression and anxiety. She made the courageous decision to begin counseling, which she found to be extremely helpful. One of the counselor's suggested coping tactics was writing. As a result, Kimber's lifestyle blog came to life: The Kimberz.com. Like so many others, she found that personal blogging has real benefits. Some of the gains result in direct healing from trauma as well as personal growth. Sharing difficult personal experiences and pain can connect a blogger to others who experience similar feelings and anxiety. In the process of sharing with others, the blogger can reduce her sense of isolation as well as providing support for readers. Kimber found all of these to be true and has continued her blog throughout her healing journey. She shares her challenges in domestic and personal stories, which provide hope for others by inspiring them to recognize their own power and purpose as well as resilience in difficult times.

Kimber's primary business focus is LeNoire Sugar, the family-owned business with its roots in love that was founded in 2020. In the midst of the global pandemic when everyone was advised to remain at home, Kimber found herself in need of a pedicure. Leaving her home for a pedicure was not an option, even if salons had been open. Her creative (and thoughtful) husband, using his creative culinary skills, created a lemon and sugar scrub for her without her knowledge. His initiative, followed by a deluxe personal pedicure using the scrub, triggered the birth of a new product line and their new business venture. Their first product, the foot scrub, was conceived using only natural ingredients available in their kitchen.

As they co-created more of the product and refined the ingredients, they purchased containers and distributed the scrub to family and friends, asking for feedback. Kimber's sisters fell in love with the scrub and promoted it on social media. Without the benefit of a website or a product line name, the word spread, and others purchased the scrub. With worldwide skincare sales of over $200 billion per year, the market is always wide open to new products, especially distinctive ones. Kimber knew that her product was unique. Not only did she use all-natural ingredients, but this was a family-originated, family-owned, infused-with-love business. Building a brand based on these attributes would be the essential brand identity for the product line. She believed that customers would fall in love with the personality as well as the effectiveness of the product. She set to work to build the brand through packaging, a unique name and the story behind the line.

With all beauty lines, the business name, logo and packaging are the most important initial decisions to make. Along with birthing the original product in the line, Kimber and her husband also collaborated on the business and product names. Proud of their Black heritage and embracing all things French, they chose the name LeNoire Sugar.

Early on in the business, they were able to provide local spas and outlets with the scrubs, followed by lip balms and body butters. Since the initial launch of the line, Kimber and her husband have developed a men's line along with women's products, both with a focus on melanated skin. A children's line was created after Kimber formulated a natural and safe product for the treatment of her children's eczema. Kimber had concerns about the long-term use of topical steroid creams for treatment, so she decided to create her own safe product. She is confident that her customers can use all of her products without worrying about skin sensitivities or allergies. Knowing that she is benefiting the wellness of others is a big motivator for her as is her sister, Sharon. Sharon is a role model and has been the biggest cheerleader for Kimber personally and in business.

Kimber's products are sold not only to create a revenue stream but are also crafted to help others. The element of love with which the first product was created is intentionally infused in all the products. Kimber is on a mission to fulfill her purpose in life. She firmly believes that God placed her on earth to be an agent of change and in service to others. All of her activities and all of her efforts are centered around the enrichment of life for her family and her community.

As a member of Black Women in Business in Austin, Kimber first asked how she could be of help to the organization before looking to benefit personally as a business owner. When she learned of the food drive during the pandemic to provide groceries for those who needed assistance, she offered to volunteer time in the food pickup and distribution efforts. Along with providing help for the organization, Kimber received support provided by the membership. Being able to interact with and be mentored by other Black women as she grew her skincare business was invaluable. A vendor fair organized by BWIB introduced her to many other women and businesses who have become customers, sponsors and allies of LeNoire Sugar. Opportunities for growth would not have come without the involvement with Black Women in Business.

Kimber's advice to other women who are juggling responsibilities and creative passions is to find such a group of women to help with the tasks where an owner's talents may be lacking. To have people acting as supporters and mentors is essential. She believes that if every woman had faith in herself and her abilities completely, she could achieve whatever she set out to do. She is a woman of power and a woman of love, the two gracefully intertwined to create a business with heart.

59

MCGILL

#THEEXCHANGE

YVETTE DENISE MCGILL is a multitasking woman fiercely focused on a personal mission—service to others through her writing and speaking brand #theEXCHANGE. She harnesses her talents, wisdom and resilience to uncover and rediscover with others in their times of challenge, modeling this in her early life as well as adulthood. Yvette is a strong wife, mother and grandmother who inspires audiences. Through storytelling, she shares how a challenging childhood was overcome. Encouraging others to accept themselves, she walks alongside them as they transform into loving and happy adults.

Yvette was born in La Marque, Texas, as what she considers the "best of George and Rhody Ward." Her childhood years were difficult, which she believes caused her to become an unhappy adult. Although an abusive mother caused her much pain, she credits a caring father for providing her the lessons in love, which she passes on through her coaching wisdom.

"Exchanging my truth for your transformation."

At eighteen when she discovered she was pregnant, Yvette married and moved out of state. Stresses of life as a newlywed can multiply when a baby occupies a prominent space in the family, and Yvette experienced loneliness. Living far from family with no support system added further tensions to Yvette's personal life. She subsequently divorced and moved with her baby to Texas, where she struggled as a single mom. Having multiple jobs made it difficult to care for her daughter as she would have liked. A new relationship with a man who offered safety and security led to marriage and another daughter. Upon her return to Texas, Yvette also reconnected with her mother, who became a loving grandmother to her girls, demonstrating a love and kindness that Yvette had not felt as a child. As she observed the tenderness her mom surprisingly showed her daughters, she was reminded of her own childhood, which had lacked affection. She understood that people change as they mature, and she found forgiveness for how her mom treated her as a child.

Yvette's marriage of twenty-three years to her second husband was not the solid, happy relationship it appeared to those outside her family. Although she felt she was in a loveless relationship, she was grateful for the close connection with her older sister, who had always acted as a mother figure to her. Research shows that a lack of parental affection in childhood makes it difficult to deeply connect with others in adulthood. Experiencing love from a close family member does offset this childhood trauma, yet it is still difficult to develop deep bonds with others. As Yvette ended her second marriage, she began a journey of self-reflection and self-love, and this is when she believes she began to heal.

Yvette credits her faith in God as the key to building a life with love and purpose. For many years, she felt as though she lived a "dream deferred." Her

hunger for a more fulfilling life of purpose overpowered her fears and sadness. She realized that she had lived most of her life caring for others' needs first and herself last. She was a wife, mother and stepmother, but didn't really know the real Yvette. As her second marriage ended, she discovered innate talents not being used. With resilience and a sense of purpose, she used her talents of coaching and support to help others. If it was her intention to provide, she knew that she needed to love herself as a part of God's purpose for her.

Yvette began to share her real and raw story of childhood trauma with women's church groups. Her audiences were grateful to know they were not alone in their suffering. As Yvette grew stronger in her faith and in her resolve to know herself, her childhood sweetheart joined her church, and they were eventually married. Yvette believes that all of her next steps were led by God as she forgave her mom and asked for understanding from her daughter for any faults in parenting. She was led to write her first book as she listened more deeply to divine messages. As long as Yvette listened to the Universe speaking to her, her health began to improve. Encouraged by her pastor, she continued with a forgiveness practice, showing grace to various family members.

During this time of self-discovery, Yvette was working in corporate America. Her new husband encouraged her to follow her heart and do work in an environment that called to her. She founded a daycare center where she worked with her daughter daily, which brought them closer, healing some old wounds.

As Yvette continued doing speaking engagements, she developed a keen interest in telling her story in written form as well. As her writing took shape, she was encouraged by a book editor to pursue writing and speaking full time, so she made the difficult decision to follow where her heart led and closed the doors to the daycare center in January 2020.

Yvette is now a proud author of six books. The titles include *Boss'd Up On Purpose*, *#theEXCHANGE*, *It's Not That Easy—Stop Telling Me to Get Over It*, *Soulful Prayers*, *#theEXCHANGEcontinues* and *Soulful Affirmations*. Pursuing an idea to create a conference for fifty friends for her fiftieth birthday, Yvette began a more intentional professional speaking venture of her own.

Although #theEXCHANGE is Yvette's primary focus, she also is the CEO of Malachi Management LLC, a company that focuses on helping individuals regain control of their lives. As a trained anger management specialist with Malachi Management, Yvette offers classes that provide resources for anger management, parenting and domestic violence prevention. Yvette is a certified life coach through Les Brown University, which supports her work in Malachi Management. Additionally, Yvette and her husband jointly own a business called Our2Scents, crafting fragrances, colognes and air fresheners. She and her husband have distributors in several states.

As a member of Black Women in Business, Yvette is an advocate for all women who have dreams of independence as entrepreneurs. She believes that the resilience she has experienced throughout her life is found in all of the members and their life stories. She knows that the members' stories are not their identities; like her, they are a part of their past and not their future.

Katii
MCKINNEY

AND CROWNED, LLC

STUDIES SHOW THAT THE NUMBER ONE reason businesses fail is because there is no market need. Katii McKinney, CEO and Founder of And Crowned, LLC saw a problem where there was a need and set out to respond. In 2017, she recognized a gap in the beauty product market that was going unresolved and took action. A visit to a beauty supply store sparked an idea that was soon to be birthed as a business. And with support from mentors in Black Women in Business, she has thrived.

Katii McKinney grew up in New Braunfels, Texas, graduating from New Braunfels High School and then continuing her education at Prairie View A&M. She graduated with a bachelor's degree in computer science. This was followed by a master's degree from Walden University in information systems management with a concentration in business management. Katii considers herself deeply rooted in her community in New Braunfels and has always called this community home.

"It can take time to undo negative feelings."

When Katii was unable to find a position in her field with hours that were in sync with her role as a mom, she took a position in customer service. Her husband was in the military and during his deployment, she took full responsibility for all of the family duties and worked full time.

An avid learner, Katii used her sense of curiosity to learn everything she could about each company that employed her. She was curious and eager to know everything about not only her position but all operational procedures for any segment of the business with which she interacted. Working with Animal Supply Company, located in Central Texas, Katii took the same eager-to-learn approach. Curiosity about all business operations was a driving force. She knew that it was possible to provide unsurpassed customer service the more she knew—from the top down to the most basic of operations.

Katii believes that everything she learned, from e-commerce, order processing, purchasing, warehouse operations to shipping, has since served her well in her own business. She also believes that she landed in the right place at the right time in order to learn what she would need for the future. Management was very willing to teach her everything she needed to be an excellent employee and more.

Building a business was not intuitive for Katii. She did not grow up in an entrepreneurial family environment. Neither her parents nor her grandparents owned or managed businesses, and she had no business role models as a youngster living at home. She understands that she received a valuable education in supply chain management while employed at Animal Supply Company. This would become the organizational foundation for the launch of her own beauty supply business.

While working full time in customer service for Animal Supply Company, Katii developed all of the essential infrastructure for her online beauty shopping platform. She also observed how the business developed from a family business serving local customers to a much larger distribution company. While establishing her own business platform, Katii launched her website with funding she received from family. Some of the original beauty products she offered on her website have continued to grow with her. She has sourced products that are not only the best in the industry, but that are produced by family-owned businesses. Katii admires the camaraderie and closeness of families in business together.

Why did she choose to focus on beauty products, and specifically, why hair care? Katii has two teenage daughters who as children didn't like their hair. This translated into an increasing lack of self-esteem, which was disturbing to their mom. Katii researched styles and products, then sought advice from retailers who did not have the answers Katii was seeking. Negative feelings about hair are pervasive in the Black community, and Katii wanted to change this attitude. By sourcing and researching products that provide positive results, she was able to select brands that could change attitudes toward hair. Katii's hair and skin care product supply line, operating under the umbrella company And Crowned LLC, is named Elegant and Dapper. The target market for her products is the Black community or anyone with curly hair who looks for results—men and women, heads or beards. That casual visit to a beauty supply store was enlightening to Katii. Many products were offered, but the staff had not tried them and did not know how they performed. Katii knew she could do better.

All of the products sourced and sold on the And Crowned website have been personally tested by Katii or someone in her family. Only the best of the best makes it to her virtual "shelves." She represents many small brands that provide excellent results but don't have large marketing budgets. Products that her family tested and which don't meet their stringent standards are not represented by And Crowned LLC.

Katii is proud of her daughters, who have important roles in her business. Not only were they the inspiration for developing an online store, but they are also very involved in product testing and selection. The girls help in the marketing and sales side of the business as well. Katii has seen her daughters' self-esteem and confidence increase as they participate in growing the family company, especially as they provide useful advice and support for social media.

In the near future, as a part of the And Crowned brand, Katii will host events featuring the products she represents as well as hair fashion shows for the San Antonio area. Typically, these events are held in larger cities such as Dallas, and she wants to develop a venue for local stylists to provide education and showcase their talents.

Resilience is essential in business. Challenges are part of the normal course of events and the savvy business owner will always need to roll with the punches. As a global pandemic affected the world, marketing events that Katii had planned were canceled. Because her online presence was established by 2020, Katii was able to ramp up virtual marketing quite easily. Fortunately, as COVID-19 restrictions declined, events were rescheduled.

Resilience in adulthood often stems from overcoming challenges as a child. When contemplating the source of mental toughness in building business, one can look back at the same traits early in life. Katii was the only Black girl in her grade at school, and she had many struggles associated with that. As a first grader, her teacher did not want to assist her because she was not reading at the same level as other students. In spite of this, Katii did learn and found that she could become an advocate for her own learning throughout her life. The tenacious little girl who was ignored for not being able to read went on to complete bachelor's and master's degrees and build a successful family-owned business today.

Terry MITCHELL

BLACK LEADERS COLLECTIVE

We are in the midst of a social justice era. Concern for the equitable distribution of wealth, opportunities and privileges lies with individuals while it is also a growing concern within the corporate arena. Any community is fortunate to have forward-thinking leaders such as Terry Mitchell in their midst to accelerate awareness and action.

Terry grew up in East Austin, as the oldest of three sisters. Her parents had immigrated from Trinidad and Tobago in order to improve the opportunities for their family. Although not well-off in assets, Terry feels she has always been rich in love. Her mother especially had a strong influence on her life and future successes. Mom placed a strong emphasis on education for her family and went to extraordinary lengths to secure spots for her daughters in schools where their potential would be nurtured. After high school graduation, Terry attended and graduated from the University of Texas at Austin, majoring in corporate communications.

"Education has been my saving grace."

Terry also credits her mother with being a model of activism and advocacy. She learned the importance of giving back to those who are underserved. As a child, Terry recalls individuals in need being housed in their home on a temporary basis. Mom taught social responsibility and shared the importance of following the lead of lessons from Dr. Martin Luther King Jr. and Malcolm X. The lessons in Terry's childhood home also included appreciation of heritage and the importance of being a proud Black girl, now a woman. These messages created a family proud of their heritage and eager to lift up those who were experiencing challenges. The love of community service taught by Terry's mom is now a motivating force in her personal and professional life.

Terry's brainchild, Black Leaders Collective, is a collaboration of more than eighty Central Texas leaders representing grassroots community members, nonprofit leaders, entrepreneurs, artists, activists, educators, policymakers, and young professionals. This movement is intersectional as well as intergenerational. Everyone must have a seat at the table when change is discussed. The BLC is open to the support of all leaders and allies in Travis and Williamson Counties, with a mission of service, advocacy and amplification of the Black community. As Founder, Terry is proud of the coalition, which has come together to create positive change for today and the future.

As an organizer of the peaceful protest of 15,000 individuals in Austin following the death of George Floyd, Terry came to realize that Black leaders of local groups were not collectively working together around issues. As a part of the debrief following the protest, the question arose, "What happens next?"

Following the protest, Terry proposed that Black leaders communicate and work together as a coalition to create change. Forty leaders initially began

these conversations. These leaders included elected officials, nonprofit leaders, business owners and community grassroots leaders. Two concerns rose to the forefront. The most significant matter, recognized by the Black male leaders, was the need for collective therapy. There was a need to examine how racism had shown up in the minds, bodies and souls of the community. The collective began and yielded almost immediate results, with less power hoarding and sabotage of individual efforts. A second result was the recognition of the need to solidify a vision for what Black Austin should look like in the next seven generations. The original leaders sought to work on the current issues while forward thinking into the future. The leaders shaped a vision for the community that focused on health, education, economic and workforce development, housing, transportation, culture, arts and entertainment. In less than eight months, governmental entities passed three policies, illustrating the power of collective efforts. Issue groups meet monthly, with the entire collective meeting bimonthly to continue the work.

Even with the commitment of time and energy to Black Leaders Collective, Terry also serves as the Chief Operating Officer of E & Co Tech, a boutique software development firm. The ten-year-old company, which she co-owns with her husband, primarily serves governmental agencies. Terry is also the owner of Austin Socialite, which produces social impact events such as Urban Health Expo, Pitch Black Austin and the Austin Icon Awards. Their website is an entertainment information resource for city happenings. Terry is also the co-founder of the three-year-old Glam Beauty Bar. She views the salon as an incubator, educating stylists in the business side of the industry with hopes that they will advance to become owners of their own businesses one day. She is training the next entrepreneurs of the future. Terry is also the Managing Partner of EveryBODY Yoga Studio.

As a member of Black Women in Business she is delighted to be among those who think alike, who have similar backgrounds and are welcoming to others. She has found the organization to be extremely supportive and helpful in finding collaborations, funding sources, business advice and camaraderie. Speaking the same language of business is valuable. Women business owners can find themselves isolated and have no one that understands specific issues. Having cheerleaders and a team around you is beneficial for women who strive to bring their dreams into reality.

Terry is not hesitant in stating her pride in being a strong Black woman. She honors resilience as a trait of all Black women. With challenges and with lack, women become creative and exhibit strength of character. Resilience should not be considered a negative, seen only through the lens of victimhood. She views it from a place of strength and power.

Her advice to anyone thinking of starting a business is to think of business as a journey. She advises women to start from wherever they are and to stay the course. She is also an avid learner and advises all future business owners to do the same. Take in as much information as possible from every source. Learn from everyone. Learn from those with wisdom and experience, but also seek advice from the younger generation. They know how to market, and they know how to connect. Finally, Terry stresses the importance of mission. Knowing one's purpose and the purpose of the business is critical to ultimate success. Based upon the drive and the mission of every endeavor that Terry touches, she is discernibly and visibly living her purpose to the gain of every life she touches.

Patricia (Pat) MOORE

N-V-Us Fashions and Boutique

SHOPPING, WHETHER ONLINE or in person, is a national pastime. With the rise of e-commerce, it's only natural that the number of online shoppers worldwide rises along with it. Although numbers vary, it is estimated that in 2021 the number of online buyers was 2.14 billion, which means that one in four people in the world buy online. This number grows every year. Patricia (Pat) Moore has been a shopper for as long as she can recall. She is one of the 75% of people in the world who have always made purchases in brick-and-mortar stores. She doesn't just like it—she loves it. And as so many entrepreneurs before her have done, she has turned her passion into a thriving business.

As a girl, Pat shopped with her mom. She believes this strongly influenced her love of shopping as an adult. Growing up an only child, she had a lot of opportunity to learn from and be influenced by her dad, who was a clever and industrious entrepreneur. Not only was he a pastor in the family church, but he also held a full-time position at Carbide Chemical

"Find your passion and make it a business."

until his retirement. Additionally, he built a thriving disposal business in their rural community near Galveston, Texas. Post-retirement, the business continued, and Patricia was able to see firsthand the work ethic required to keep a business successful.

As an adult, Pat's husband admonished her that her love of shopping and finding the perfect bargain might be "getting out of hand." Pat listened, but was a little baffled, wondering how something that could be so enjoyable for her might ever be considered too much. Because shopping was such an anxiety reliever for Pat, she hated the thought of curtailing the activity that she loved. Retail therapy is a real thing. When we shop, the "feel good hormone" dopamine is released. In addition, the human brain loves to make comparisons. In shopping, we use data that we observe in society (what other people are buying) and use it to compare to offerings in stores or online. The relational brain activity is not only stimulating, but pleasurable.

In sharing her husband's observation with her sister and best friend, Donna, Pat considered the option of taking her passion and turning it into profit by shopping for wearables for others. As an entrepreneur himself, Pat's husband had always encouraged his wife to consider working for herself. His advice was to find something she loved and then create an outlet for it. Shopping was never difficult or unpleasant for her. She found that looking and storing retail information (more brain-stimulating comparisons) was just as pleasurable as actually making purchases. Converting her passion into a business seemed like a good move.

In 2010, prior to starting the business, which she named N-V-Us Fashions and Boutique, Pat was a project manager for a printing company. During that

time, she did "research" by actively shopping for herself. She traveled for her job as project manager, and off-the-clock shopping was always a part of each trip. One of her favorite distance boutiques was in Atlanta. On one trip, she took the opportunity to quiz the owner on her business operations. Pat gained valuable information about purchasing, operations, marketing and sales that she would find useful when she opened her own boutique.

Within a few weeks of her Atlanta visit, her sister and favorite co-conspirator in launching the business notified Pat that she had set an appointment for the two of them to meet with clothing and shoe representatives in Dallas at the Dallas Market Center. At the meeting, they discussed a supplier arrangement for the soon-to-be-launched boutique. Initially, Pat planned to sell shoes; however, after the meeting, she added clothing to her boutique inventory as well. The plans for the new business venture were fully underway with the completion of necessary applications, paperwork and licenses.

For the first year, 2010, Pat marketed and sold through events, pop-up shops and a designated space within a salon in San Antonio. As the business grew, Pat made the move to a storefront in a local shopping mall, where she also planned and produced fashion shows. She continued to have fashion shows every three months, finding that on these event days, sales would climb. Music and the excitement of a live event built interest. In the second year of her fashion business, she made the decision to leave her full-time job as project manager. By 2013, Pat moved to an online-only sales platform and closed the shop in the mall. While she was building the new infrastructure for an online-only business, she rejoined the workforce as an insurance agent to supplement the family income.

Growing the social media presence of N-V-Us Boutique has been a large focus for Pat, and she has engaged a brand ambassador who also helps her to grow her follower numbers. Currently, she receives orders from Facebook as well as her online store.

Being resilient to market changes, life changes and business changes are essential to owning one's own business. Pat felt challenged when she faced the unplanned closing of her busy mall storefront. A pivot from plan A to plan B caused doubt and fear that she had made some wrong moves. Her husband had encouraged her to build up her online presence for many months prior to the store closing, and she felt regret for not acting sooner. By the time 2020 arrived, Pat's online presence was active, and she was pleased that she had no physical shop to concern her.

Because Pat had refined her record keeping and business practices during her business' brick-and-mortar year, when financial support applications were required for emergency funding in 2020, Pat was prepared. Her applications only took minutes to complete. She also transitioned from direct to drop shipping, reducing the need for large inventory. This business practice has allowed the business to accelerate growth and reduce costs. Personal resilience is also familiar to Pat. Traumas in her teen years and early married life were met with grit and grace, similar to what she displayed in her business years.

Pat has learned countless lessons through her journey as an entrepreneur. Being a part of Black Women in Business has been a significant part of her support system. Coaching, advice and camaraderie are key ingredients to starting and growing a successful venture, and BWIB has provided all of these abundantly.

Tonya
NIXON
TRAVIS COUNTY CONSTABLE

THERE ARE SOME PEOPLE YOU MEET who immediately make you smile. Surprisingly, one of central Texas' elected officials is one of those people. Tonya Nixon has the distinction of being the first Black female to run for and win the elected position of constable in Travis County. In 2020, she was sworn into office after receiving 60% of the vote in the primary election, which meant there was no need for a runoff. Not only is she the first Black female to run and win this seat in Travis County, but she is also the first to achieve this honor in all of Central Texas. Although elected officials in the State of Texas are increasingly diverse, there still remains an extremely small number of women serving and an even smaller number of women of color. Communities, as well as businesses, want their leaders to look like them and to represent them. As a native of Austin and a native of the community that she represents (East Austin), she serves her community and Precinct One within as well as outside of the area she serves. She is involved in official County issues as a part of her duties, as well as being a servant leader on her own time.

"The community is my passion."

Tonya is the third child in a family of six children. She primarily lived with her grandmother, who provided stability and structure that she had not had in her mother's home. In her senior year of high school, she learned that she was pregnant, and soon after graduation, she left home to be independent and await the birth of her son. As a single mother, there were challenges. Her dream was to go to college and become a peace officer. As a new mother with responsibilities, life had other plans for her, and she chose to take a job at the IRS as a data transcriber. She worked not only to provide for her son as well as her siblings, who were still living at home. Talented and fast on the keyboard, she excelled in her position, even though the dream to serve her community as a peace officer continued to tug at her mind and heart.

Austin Community College opened a campus in East Austin, which allowed Tonya to attend evening classes while she worked full time for the IRS. She was highly motivated to provide for herself and her son. As an extremely competitive person, Tonya continually challenged herself to do better, do more, and to improve herself, her dream compelling her to succeed. Even as she worked for the IRS and attended evening classes, she also worked for IBM.

Highly motivated to make her dream a reality, in 2016, Tonya became a reserve police officer in the constable's office. Finding a position suitable for a single, working mom in law enforcement was not easy; however, the constable's office seemed a good fit even though, as a reservist, there was no salary. As a police reservist, Tonya performed part-time policing functions on a voluntary basis. But the fit was good, and the dream became a reality. Nights were long, yet Tonya was dedicated.

Although her intention was to stay at the constable's office only until she completed her college coursework, she realized that the community policing she loved could be found there.

After completing coursework at Austin Community College, Tonya entered a competition for single moms to win a full-ride scholarship to Virginia College. At the same time, she was the sole source of support and encouragement for her son, who was struggling in high school. Her focus was to ensure that he completed his high school education, which meant that she wasn't able to complete her coursework at Virginia College. She chose family first. She was determined to provide the type of quality support she lacked when she struggled in her own high school experience. This period of time was not easy for her.

Psychological resilience is the ability to cope mentally or emotionally with stressful situations and return to pre-crisis behavior. Women are often called upon to look inward and draw upon innate resilience, whether in a family setting or in the workplace. It is challenging to soldier on when we feel like things are out of control. Tonya has been faced with making tough decisions within her own family. When substance abuse and personal danger became commonplace for her son and as he moved in and out of trouble, she knew it was necessary to surrender him to the authorities. She has always made decisions on what is best for her son and is a staunch cheerleader for him. She continues to encourage him to become his best self, reminding him that his story is still being written. As a mother and a peace officer, she works in the field of infinite optimism touched with a hit of reality. In that way, she sees the everyday for what it is, but believes in the goodness of man. Pure resilience.

Community policing was the dream, yet the opportunity to make a larger impact presented itself to Tonya when she was encouraged to run for the office of Travis County Constable. Running for office was important to Tonya not only because she felt she had even more service she might perform in the community, but she also wanted to demonstrate to members of her "home" community that there are numerous ways that they could become involved and make a difference. As a woman from their "hood," she wanted to exhibit to residents in a way that everyone could be welcomed at the table. Encouraging everyone to have a voice, to speak up and to improve the quality of life for all, is important to Tonya.

As the recipient of numerous community awards, Constable Nixon is also a frequent invited speaker. In a talk given at the Ann Richards School for Girls, Tonya advised the students to believe in themselves, work hard to achieve their dreams and not to try to fit a mold because following one's own passions is most important. She counsels them to reach for their dreams and to work without letting anyone's judgment get in the way. Hold true to your own beliefs, she encourages them—start young and don't waste time. Tonya is a woman who lives as she advises. She doesn't waste a second of her time and makes the most of every moment.

Dineen PARKER

ACROSS THE STITCH

WHAT DO THE TRAINING AND LEADING of military troops and the delicate craft of cross-stitch have in common? A lot, as entrepreneur Dineen Parker can tell you. Two years out of high school, she joined the military in order to serve her country and to expand her life experiences. And along the way, fine needlework joined the effort.

Dineen was born in Jersey City, New Jersey. As a toddler, her parents relinquished custody of her to her great aunt, who raised her through high school. Her biological parents died when she was seventeen, which further compounded existing abandonment issues she experienced. After high school graduation, Dineen attended college for two years before choosing to join the military. When asked, the majority of recruits like Dineen cite the call to serve, adventure and travel and the benefits as primary reasons for enlisting.

Following training as a medic, Dineen found a significant amount of free time at her first duty station. She searched out

"Figure out what you are good at and what you enjoy."

ways to occupy her spare time, and while browsing at a crafting store, she found attractive cross-stitch kits, a craft she had never tried. With her first few kits, she didn't feel motivated to complete them, so she moved on to sewing, and this time finishing the projects she'd begun. During her early military career, she began to date her future husband, also a member of the military, who loved her and her authenticity. She made no special efforts to woo him or impress him, which made her even more attractive in his eyes. Eventually, they married.

Hobbies and leisure-time activities were put on hold as Dineen began military lab tech training in Texas and her husband was assigned to Germany. After she was transferred to Germany, they had a daughter. After both were reassigned to the US, they had another daughter and Dineen became a lab tech instructor as the couple moved to Texas for their final military placement. And after twenty-two years in the military, Dineen retired with thoughts of once again taking up the hobby she had given up in her early military career. She revived her cross-stitching and found that her days were consumed with needlework projects. Cross-stitch gave way to hand embroidery. Friends and family encouraged her to market the crafts she was making. She sold her completed projects and eventually found she had an even greater audience with the designs for the needlework she created. She discovered that her own original designs were more satisfying for her to stitch and that she was more likely to complete a project if she had also designed it.

Many individuals sell their crafts and original creations through the website Etsy. The business model allows Etsy to make money only when the seller makes a sale. There are millions of buyers who shop on this website daily. She is one of approximately 7.5 million sellers from 234 countries who find a marketplace for their creations. Etsy has over four billion dollars in sales each year, with many

sellers able to consider the revenue earned equivalent to a full-time salary. Etsy offers assistance through seller tools and services in order to help generate more sales, and Dineen took advantage of these. She continues to sell her creations through Etsy as she learns the ins and outs of online retail.

As she grew her online presence, a friend suggested that a venue for Dineen's crafts might be Extravaganza, an annual conference and vendor market sponsored annually by the Black Women in Business in Austin. She applied for a vendor space and sold a significant amount of her needlework. She also received orders for custom work. Being new to business, Dineen was not familiar with pricing structures and did not know how to price the products she created and sold. She knew that she covered her material costs; however, she soon realized that she did not account for her time and any overhead involved. Although new business owners often set pricing at either what people will pay or what the seller would be willing to pay for a product or service, this is not a sustainable model. Through her membership in Black Women in Business and through lessons learned from mentors, Dineen soon recognized the changes needed and took corrective action.

As she began to exhibit at more local events, she purchased a high-performance embroidery machine. She moved from 100% hand stitching to a volume approach. Then the global pandemic arrived and shifted business worldwide as well as at home. Dineen quickly pivoted. When asked if she could produce masks for Black Women in Business, Dineen agreed to provide them for the organization as well as for her Etsy marketplace. As the demand for masks slowed, she looked for other markets for all of her creations. Demand for cross-stitch crafts was slowing, although the patterns she made and sold were still popular.

During a visit to a local fabric store, she noticed some small tents nearby where vendors were selling their wares in outdoor markets. She realized that although opportunities to sell in indoor markets were rare, outdoor venues were still viable even as restrictions during the pandemic were lifted. She sought out and sold at outdoor venues. Her skills using her high-speed embroidery machine grew as well. After Dineen discovered an embroidery peer group who shared ways to promote her business, her sales grew. Business expanded as she created a large number of personalized pieces. Her visibility in the marketplace increased, and she had more requests to make products for other businesses. Caps, shirts and jackets with business logos were soon a large part of her product line. The high-speed embroidery machine she had could not adequately handle certain items and their logos, so she upsized to a commercial machine that could handle the production. Commercial orders now account for a vast percentage of Dineen's business.

Resilience appears in many forms. On occasion, it is said that bouncing back from adversity is the ultimate manifestation of resilience; however, a pivot from one fading product line to one that emerges as a superstar is also a brand of resilience. Recognition that methods for marketing and pricing no longer meet the organization's needs are signs of resilience.

Black Women in Business provides support and guidance for such pivots in all phases of business growth. As a member of BWIB, Dineen has found a close sisterhood with other women who have become friends as well as advisors. Referrals and the expansion of her reach through social media are also benefits of the supportive sisterhood. Dineen has come full circle in her life from developing a part-time hobby, setting it aside and then returning to it as a business later in life.

Shirley QUICK

Hat Lady Shirley

SUCCESSFUL RETIREMENT takes many shapes and forms. For past generations, leaving a final career often meant sleeping late, making one's own schedule, traveling or simply pursuing hobbies they never had time to pursue before. But a more contemporary type of retirement may be considered an "encore," with bonus careers occupying life along with all the other perks of not punching a time clock.

Shirley Quick, known as the Hat Lady, in recent years has developed and grown her encore career, using her creativity and organizational skills to design and sell a unique brand of hats throughout Texas. The inventory includes all styles of hats and caps. She buys various basic hats such as fedoras, sun hats and ball caps, and decorates them with "blingy" jewelry that she has sourced from thrift stores, vintage shops, jewelry stores and online sources. Seeking out stylish objects that she can break apart and use to adorn the hats, the Hat Lady creates her own designs and then uses them as inspirations for her one-of-a-kind toppers. Shirley also scours magazines

"Find education and training to start your business."

99

and may even use hats seen on television dramas such as "Downton Abbey" as inspiration. Noting that feathers were all the rage in the early part of the 20th century, she now adds them to her creations. The Hat Lady has also been known to gain inspiration from the British royal family and the hats they wear. Shirley pays attention to current styles and observes that the most popular hats women choose currently are the baseball hat and small-brimmed fedora.

Hat Lady Shirley was born in Clinton, Oklahoma, with seven siblings, and a plethora of grandparents, aunts, uncles and cousins. She knows the benefit of a large number of relatives who care for each other's needs and feels fully surrounded and supported not only by relatives but also by her growing church family. She feels blessed to have grown up in such a close-knit environment.

Reflecting upon her early years, Shirley is certain that she was influenced by her mother and all the abundant creative activities in their home. Her seamstress mom used her talents for holidays, birthdays and every imaginable occasion. Mom made decorations and gifts for family and friends while also showing off her culinary talents at numerous gatherings for family and friends. She gained the reputation as a part-time caterer for large parties.

After graduating from high school, Shirley attended nearby Southwestern State University, graduating with a BA degree in Recreational Leadership and a minor in Sociology. Her major course of study was a natural for her, and she believes that the interactive games, sports, and camping were similar to her family life.

While at college, Shirley met her future husband, who joined the military after his first year at Southwestern State. Thus began her introduction into military

life and her own career in civil service. Shirley and her husband married during her junior year of college prior to his assignment to Fort Hood in Texas. Although he relocated, Shirley remained in Oklahoma to complete her degree.

Shirley's early work life included a brief period as program director at an assisted living residence followed by a position as a substitute teacher. After their first child was born, Shirley and her husband relocated with the military to Germany. While in Germany, she accepted a civilian position with the military as a GS4 serving the Youth Services and Programs at the assigned base. She drew upon her creative background to coordinate and direct youth events. She recalls the family, school and church plans that her mother and aunt had organized and felt as though she was still following their lead. Looking back on her early years, Shirley sees these family members as role models of creativity. They could make do with very limited resources and were the inspiration for a lot of Shirley's events. As children mature and lose the sense of unabandoned creativity, they often look for cues from adults on how to be imaginative and creative in life. By having adults who model "out of the box" thinking and imaginative approaches to problem-solving, children like Shirley transform from a child of simple wonderment to adult execution of multiple styles.

After the tour of duty in Germany, Shirley returned to the US and separated from her husband. She continued to work with the government, completing forty years of service with a final move to Killeen, Texas, as a relocation specialist for the military. Following her move back to Texas, Shirley's mom moved from Oklahoma to be with Shirley and to assist with childcare. Shirley describes her house after her mom's arrival as a "craft house" because it was filled with copious amounts of craft materials for home décor. Through her mom's influence, she began her own crafting journey. She discovered unique ways to decorate home goods as well as wearables. Through research, she learned about the dates and locations of pop-up events in central Texas, where she sold her creations. As soon as she retired from the military, Shirley pursued her business with passion, traveling to numerous shows each year.

Keeping with family tradition, Shirley's teenage granddaughter has now joined her as an assistant in working the shows. She participates in all operations except for the construction of the hats. Shirley enjoys teaching the next generation how to organize and perform all sales functions.

Shirley markets her hats through social media as well as pop-up markets and other events. Research for new designs involves time spent reviewing Instagram, YouTube and Facebook groups. She also follows other media sources for ideas. Although Shirley has found social media to be the biggest challenge to her as a small business owner, she fully embraced the opportunity to learn how to conquer it. She has an active presence on several platforms such as Facebook and Instagram, where she features her designs.

Education is important to Shirley. She has attended numerous classes and webinars in order to stay on top of her marketing tactics. As a savvy businesswoman, she understands that people prefer to buy online, and wants to stay current. In the future, Shirley plans to work with a marketing consultant to help her identify her target audience and sell to them. Social media will become Shirley's new frontier for learning to sell. Additionally, the reduction of shipping costs is on her radar for improvement.

As a member of Black Women in Business, she enjoys the network of friends and the opportunity to learn from them. As a seasoned businesswoman, she also has much to give back to others. No matter what age or stage of life, enthusiasm and curiosity serve us well in inspiring us to start a business, learn a new skill or train a young family member. Attitude is everything.

Anye
SMITH

Veh's Treats and Eats

RESILIENCE IS OFTEN THOUGHT OF as a one-time occurrence. Something unexpected happens, and in that moment, there is an active choice or even an unconscious effort to bounce back, to survive in the midst of what might seem like the darkest night of the soul. During traumatic events, many women find it possible to dig deep and lean on that incomparable will to survive and thrive. Sometimes we might be able to identify the source and sometimes resilience is just in our nature. The will to live. The will to not let the pitfalls of life control us. After unfortunate events, hitting a proverbial bottom is often the catalyst for change, for transformation.

Chef Anye Smith is a Louisiana girl born in Baton Rouge. Today's Anye is not the girl that found early life a challenge.

As a natural athlete, she became involved in cheerleading until she found basketball and basketball claimed her. Between seventh and eighth grade, she grew to her mature

"Perfecting my imperfections."

height of five feet, eleven inches. Her height was an asset, yet her innate abilities at the sport made her a sought-after player for varsity teams. She committed herself to the game and worked hard to be the best she could be. And then misfortune happened. At the beginning of her senior year, she injured her knee, which eliminated her from playing or training. Sitting on the bench was not what she signed on for. Why had the universe allowed this to happen to the young woman who had found meaning in life? She had worked extremely hard to train and get into top shape for senior year so she could be recruited for college teams. This metaphorical slap down resulted in behavioral issues which were hard to resolve.

After graduation, she attended Southern University in Baton Rouge, attending for two years before she decided to relocate to Texas to be closer to family.

As she was in the process of recentering herself, other blows came. The death of her cousin Javeh, who was more like a brother to her, affected Anye deeply, sending her into a state of depression. Additionally, the death of her dear grandmother compounded her sense of helplessness. Substance abuse and subsequent poor choices came as the result of her depression, yet arriving at this dark place where hope was lacking provided the resolve to begin to make changes in her life. She had children at this point, and she realized that she wanted to do better and be better for them.

Anye had the beginnings of an idea for her own business but without a solid plan of what it might be. After finding herself low on funds when one of her children asked for a specialty birthday cake, she taught herself how to create a Spiderman cake. Family and friends encouraged her to design and craft other cakes and offer them for sale. At that time, the business idea was born. Initially, she sold to family and friends, who encouraged her to broaden her market. As she began to develop her business plan, she knew she wanted to name her business in honor of her beloved cousin. Veh's Treats and Sweets was born.

Knowing that there was only so much she could learn on her own, Anye made the decision to accelerate her education and enroll in Le Cordon Bleu College of Culinary Arts, receiving her degree in pastry. After graduation, she continued to hold a full-time job as she worked to grow her business, which she had renamed to Veh's Treats and Eats. Her menu of items to prepare and cater had expanded beyond cakes and pastries.

In the time after graduation, Anye became pregnant and delivered a son prematurely, which put an abrupt halt to business growth and expansion. The baby presented with significant congenital heart issues as well as chromosomal abnormalities, which have caused numerous hospital stays and surgeries. Raising children at home, and managing the care of an ill newborn, have made it difficult to nurture a fledgling business. Anye felt as though she had lost the passion and drive needed for it. So many personal challenges caused her progress to slow.

If the issues with a special needs child were not enough to put a halt to business, a global pandemic arrived to completely stop orders on specialty foods on Anye's menu. With the easing of COVID-19 restrictions, Anye returned to a full-time culinary position at a regional hospital and experienced a reignited passion for her business. She has partnered with a local business to provide some of her specialty Cajun dishes for customers. Gumbo and crawfish are the most popular on her menu of dishes she prepares and sells through a partnering business. Additionally, Anye continues to receive cake orders on her own, as well as being an overflow provider for a local bakery who refers to her.

While in the past Anye participated in vendor events, the majority of her orders now are arriving either as repeat customers, referrals or from social media.

Anye is a proud member and supporter of Black Women in Business. She credits the organization with providing her with a business education and encouragement not found anywhere else. She is grateful for all the support and information available to anyone who wants to start or grow their businesses. Anye also credits her mom with providing inspiration and being a role model for her. Sometimes when there seems to be nothing else available, hard work can get the job done. Her mom had demonstrated that for her all of her life.

The best advice she would give to other girls who want to succeed in life is to stay in school, take advantage of opportunities and keep pushing toward their goals. Anye has had numerous challenges in her life, but with each of them, she has taken the high road of resilience and tenacity to push toward her own goals. She cites her children as the reason she works hard to be the best mom and business owner she can be. Anye is a model of strength and courage.

ANYE SMITH

111

Sharon SMITH

SCULPTIVATE BODY SPA

OFTEN THE WORDS, calling, profession, job are used interchangeably; however, they are uniquely dissimilar. The term "job" usually refers to any type of employment for pay, trained or untrained, which is performed by an individual with or without personal dedication or fulfillment. A "profession" might be considered similar; however, there is usually education and training involved. A "calling" implies a strong inclination with personal emphasis on the greater good for the individual or the community. A calling toward a particular line of work starts from a place of deep drive or desire. It is not a temporary urge to pursue a line of work. It is a part of an individual emanating from nurture or nature and often, both. This calling, which is a strong sense of purpose in one's life work, will always knock on the doors of our minds and hearts until we answer. This sense of calling is ingrained in Black Women in Business's early member, Sharon Smith.

As one of four children, Sharon Smith grew up the daughter of a dedicated nurse. She watched her mother work tirelessly

"Helping others is my passion."

to respond to her own calling to serve others. Her mom's long hours, as well as intense close personal contact with her patients, did not appeal to young Sharon, and she promised herself that she would never follow in her footsteps. One of Sharon's three brothers suffered from juvenile diabetes, which required a large amount of care from Sharon's mother as well as Sharon. This intense attention furthered her resolve to avoid any career in the medical profession.

Yet, despite all this, as a caring person who always found herself in situations where she answered calls for help, she naturally gravitated toward one of the most helpful careers of all, nursing. After the difficult, premature birth of one of her sons, she decided to answer the call. Without looking back, Sharon chose to train to become a licensed vocational nurse (LVN). She first received her LVN license before serving as a home health agency director for many years.

As a healthcare professional, Sharon has always understood the importance of maintaining a healthy weight. High BMI (body mass index) can lead to heart disease, strokes, diabetes, as well as high blood pressure. Maintaining a healthy lifestyle and healthy weight can also lower the risk of many cancers. As a busy nurse and director with administrative responsibilities, Sharon noticed that her eating habits were moving in a direction that was not healthy. As she gained weight, she realized she needed to take back control of her health. At about the same time, she began to learn about body sculpting, which purported to yield positive results. Sharon did her homework and learned all she could in order to offer therapies that were noninvasive and nonsurgical and might provide aesthetic results for herself as well as others. As someone who considers the entire person and practices a holistic approach to health care, she wanted to not only work with clients on their outward appearance

but also address the underlying causes of excess weight. As a medical practitioner, she is able to discern medical issues versus psychological issues versus lifestyle choices, and approach each individually.

Founded by Sharon in 2021, Sculptivate Body Spa is located in Round Rock, Texas, and offers noninvasive body contouring and shaping. The goal of the services is to rid the body of unwanted excess fat and to tighten loose skin to create a toned appearance. Sculptivate does not merely address the exterior appearance of the body. During the initial intake, Sculptivate takes an extensive health history and discusses the individual's feelings about current health and weight issues. This thorough assessment allows Sharon to determine if her services are appropriate or if outside assistance and advice from other practitioners is needed. Any medical concerns are referred to the client's health provider. Any emotional issues would also be referred to outside counseling. A treatment plan with a treatment team of one or more is set, following a discussion with the client of realistic short- and long-term goals. Using various modalities, Sharon can assist the client in improving wellness through weight loss and improved body image.

Sculptivate Body Spa addresses all mind/body/spirit issues in a highly personalized way. Although in 2022, Sculptivate only offers basic shaping and contouring methods, future plans include a wider range of services and treatments for the total health and well-being of the whole body. In addition, Sharon will provide communication and support through a Sculptivate app.

Resilience has many faces. Throughout the process of building a business, owners often embody more than one. During the pandemic and before, Sharon was able to open her body spa and take the time to complete her

RN training. Never being one to be without plans and dreams, Sharon also had previously created another business that was not yet launched, Divine Faithful Hands. This home health care provider offers integrative, non-skilled care. During the months when she could not provide direct care, she did an extensive amount of pro bono work. She created goody boxes that she delivered to individuals in assisted living facilities. As an independent contractor providing donations, she was able to enter the facilities and bring welcome gifts to residents. She also assisted homebound individuals by picking up and delivering food and medications to those who were unable to drive.

Sharon is a woman who clearly lives out her calling by helping others through her work. Actively engaging in the people services professions is her passion and her reason for being.

Sharon has been a member of BWIB since its inception. Longtime friends, she and CEO Rose Smith support each other's missions to serve. She enjoys the networking and the support of interacting with like-minded women in BWIB. Even though members may have similar businesses, there is mutual care and respect that she likens to a family. Sharon has used resources brought in through BWIB as well as the support of her sisters. And as a businesswoman with a big, giving heart, she enjoys the programs for community giveback.

As a businesswoman with years of experience in serving others while living out her dreams, Sharon's advice to other young women is to acknowledge each individual passion and pursue it in a business. And a final word? "If others don't understand your dreams, don't listen. Follow your heart."

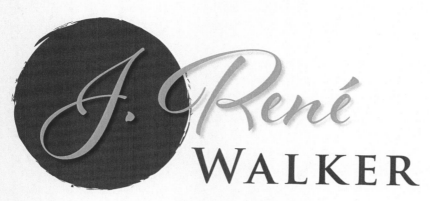

J. René WALKER

COMPASS REAL ESTATE

WOMEN WHO DO WELL in business often look back to their early careers and realize that lessons learned and skills acquired over time continue to serve them well as they move from one career to the next. J René Walker's successful career story is one of accumulated expertise, wisdom and recognition, first in the tech industry and then in real estate.

Whether relocating to new cities, changing jobs or switching careers, she has always excelled. After receiving her MBA, J. René accepted a position as a marketing executive for IBM in Boca Raton, Florida. During her years with the tech giant, she relocated eleven times, living in eleven states and gaining experience in international sales and marketing with outstanding performance in contract negotiations.

While in her first position out of college in Florida, at the age of twenty-two, she purchased her first home. As a child, she worked alongside her dad, who had a keen interest in real estate and taught her what he knew. A father, who

"Strengthen your strengths."

hoped for sons, was rewarded with daughters. His oldest, J. René, was his diminutive sidekick as he searched out real estate deals in their hometown of Philadelphia. With his favorite understudy by his side, he researched, uncovered and inspected deals that could be purchased inexpensively and rehabbed for sale. J. René observed and learned. By the time she landed in Florida as a newly minted graduate, she was ready to make her own deals. She purchased a house and set out to make it her home (after dad's approval). J. René quickly learned that the residents of her new community were unfamiliar with a woman of color living there. Their response was not welcoming. Terrorist-style acts of violence against her and her home came as a shock to her and her employer, IBM, as well. The General Manager of IBM-Boca Raton took action and put the city officials on notice. He made it known that IBM had plans to recruit the best and the brightest to work in local offices. He promised that IBM would withdraw financial support from the city, charities and real estate ventures, moving all funds and support to another nearby community if the poor treatment of their team members continued. After a period of time, J. René moved up and out, taking with her the profits from the sale of her home.

As she acquired real estate, she understood that a lot of the wealth in the Black community is tied up in home ownership. She had the knowledge and resources to acquire homes and, with each move, continued to grow her personal wealth. She realized the importance of investing in home ownership, and as her professional life grew, her personal resources did as well.

J. René learned early that resilience is a necessity for navigating any profession, especially in the C-suite. Growing up Black, growing up female and being the only one that looked like her sitting at a table of executives was often difficult. She knew the importance of being able and comfortable in oneself, and the

importance of speaking up on behalf of others. "Be my ally when I'm no longer in the room," is her admonition. J. René feels that it is important to stand up and speak up, even if it may be to one's own detriment. She sometimes found that others might not respond well to a solo female in the room, especially if she was the only Black female in the room. Advice for all women is to "know their stuff" and to strengthen their strengths. Often after years of effort to rise in the ranks to reach the C-suite, women still have to stand strong to hold their positions.

After her tenure with IBM, she moved on to work for Toshiba America and then Dell Computers, relocating four more times before settling in Round Rock, Texas. In the early 2000s, J. René decided to change careers and pursue something she knew well, real estate. She had bought and sold houses during all of her moves while in the tech industry, and she felt comfortable making this change. As she achieved success in real estate sales, she then became a broker and opened her own firm in 2004, Best Agents in Texas. When Robert Reffken of Compass learned of J. René's reputation as an industry leader, he convinced her to join his team as sales manager and then managing broker.

Along with leading a successful team at Compass, J. René serves as a mentor for students at Huston-Tillotson University and provides life lessons as well as business advice. She is an advocate for education and training for herself and her team members. The knowledge that she has amassed through three degrees and decades of experience is now used to mentor others.

What did resilience look like for J. René during COVID-19? While initially, she assumed that the real estate market might slow, just the opposite occurred. Buyers and sellers sought change. Being isolated at home caused them to realize that their current houses would not accommodate working from home or schooling children from home. Her agents were busy. J. René made every effort to be sure her agents worked safely. Compass provided educational assistance for families through an arrangement with Sylvan Learning Centers, a national chain of tutors and teachers. She believes that large offices accommodating agents and staff will never be the same again. Agents have learned to work from home or to use coffee shops for meetings. Although there is encouragement to re-engage in the office, the changes seem to be permanent.

J. René has accumulated numerous awards in her twenty years in real estate. She received the Realtor of the Year award and the Businesswoman of the Year award as chosen by the Women's Council of Realtors. She has received the designation of Educator of the Year Award for contributions to real estate education in Texas and the Platinum Top 50 Realtor Award for outstanding achievements in sales, education, industry participation and civic leadership. Most recently, she was named Executive of the Year by PT50, a realtor award program that recognizes the top Real Estate Professionals who exemplify initiative, involvement, success and philanthropy.

As a member of Black Women in Business, J. René has enjoyed an incredible amount of sharing and cooperation. Prior to joining, she found it difficult to find a group where she felt welcomed and accepted. The membership of women with different levels of business development provided her with a group of kindred spirits as well as a source for information and connection.

Colleagues and friends know J. René Walker as a woman of commitment, integrity and drive. She is a leader of many and a role model to future business leaders.

LaTonya WHITE

Traveling Made Affordable, LLC

LATONYA WHITE is a serial entrepreneur who considers education an integral part of her business and her life. As a former teacher and lead counselor, the desire to seek and share knowledge is an essential part of who she is. Her role as an educator continues in a different incarnation as an entrepreneur sharing her love of travel.

As a child growing up in Houston, Texas, LaTonya found a safe refuge from her home life in the Reserve Officers' Training Corps (ROTC). She especially credited one of her leaders who saw her for who she was and supported and nurtured her. As head of the school's ROTC program at Willowridge High School in Houston, Texas, this leader not only educated her but served as a father figure for LaTonya and many of the other students. She believes that ROTC saved her life. This organization and its leader filled a gap for many students. In academics, LaTonya never found the support she needed to achieve success. She recalls teachers who were not helpful with her learning struggles, and the

"Although I will never forget where I came from, I am so excited about where I am going."

young LaTonya of the past poses no resemblance to the successful educator, counselor and entrepreneur of today.

LaTonya is surprised at her success as a professional blogger. Initially, she began to blog as a part of her efforts to express feelings that arose due to childhood trauma. Her personal blogs led to travel blogs, and in 2018, she began to blog for festivals and was asked to contribute to a travel magazine. As her confidence and reputation grew, she left her counseling position to become a full-time blogger, and then owner of a travel business. She believes she "took the road less traveled" and has never regretted her decisions. After her first successful blogging job for FestiGals in New Orleans, she was asked to blog for Essence Festival and Mardi Gras. She looks for opportunities and says "yes" to exciting requests to share her travel insight and opinions.

Following a career as an educator, counselor and then travel blogger, LaTonya founded Traveling Made Affordable, LLC. Her business operates through Franchise Cruise Planners, and she serves as a travel agent and destination specialist. Her clients include families, newly engaged couples seeking locations for destination weddings, businesses who use travel as part of their employee incentive packages and schools in Texas that offer international and domestic field trips.

As she began her business, she found it more natural for her to take a nontraditional path. Magazine ads and other typical media didn't feel like a fit for her and didn't reflect her more personal style of communication. Tapping into what she loves best, she decided to utilize her skills on social media to promote and expand her travel business. She is up to date with technology and the uses of technology to educate and inform about travel and the dreams of

travel. She is quite comfortable being in front of the camera and uses videos to post on various platforms. As she entered her second year of business, she began a new stage of promotion, with 98% of her bookings obtained through social media. Personality, authenticity and unique delivery gained clients who enthusiastically endorse her and provide referrals.

Plans to triple her business in 2019–20 were halted when all pleasure travel stopped. Anxiety and depression overtook the typically bubby LaTonya until she looked to other skills and talents to start other revenue streams. Psychological resilience in times of despair is not easy. Using her own strength, she sought solutions to a seemingly insurmountable situation. This capability allowed her to remain calm and to move ahead with plans and economic preservation. With the relaxation of travel restrictions, LaTonya saw the industry rebound. In working with her marketing coach, she devised a new strategy to promote destination weddings. She found this pivot to be very successful. Utilizing the same authenticity and approachable demeanor, she has grown her client base once again on social media.

Resilience is LaTonya's super strength. LaTonya comes from a background of challenges, including abuse and adversity, and as a child, she felt that all the bad things that happened to her and her family would never end. As a child, she could not imagine living the life she lives today. She was led to believe by one of her teachers that she was not capable of doing math and, as a result, believed that her future was uncertain. But she has succeeded, and she is grateful. She believes that staying tough and tenacious served to get her through. One of her favorite quotes is "never say that it is impossible, because someone, somewhere is doing it."

As a believer in networking, LaTonya has found her membership in Black Women in Business to be very beneficial. Being a part of a like-minded community who can support and inspire is an essential part of the growth of every business owner. She finds it useful and inspiring to attend conferences to hear motivational speakers, especially those who remind us of our intrinsic worth. LaTonya appreciates words of encouragement and advises audiences to "be your best self and best business owner." She has seen an improvement in her relationships with others, whether they are business owners or not, and is fulfilled by the friends she has made.

As vital to LaTonya as operating a successful business is serving her community. LaTonya is the founder of an educational consulting company called Reading Beyond. She works with local schools to close the gap in reading disparity. As a former educator, she understands what is necessary to reach students and help them build their reading skills. Seeking to broaden student knowledge through experience, she provides unique trips and tours focusing on STEM educational experiences. By offering opportunities for new experiences outside of a student's neighborhood and community, she provides opportunities proven to expand their background knowledge of the world at large. She also is the owner of Wright Title, a title service company licensed by the county to assist dealerships and consumers with auto title transfers and vehicle registrations in Texas.

LaTonya suggests that every little girl today must have faith to know that though life seems horrible, she knows from experience that "your today is not your tomorrow." She counsels others to "put on your blinker and change lanes" if the life you are living is not what you desire. LaTonya did it and believes others can do the same.

WILLIAMS

WILLIAMS CAREER SCHOOL OF EXCELLENCE

LORA WILLIAMS is aware that well-educated parents generally raise children who are themselves well educated, healthier, financially stable and better off in almost every way than children without the benefit of education. Lora Williams knew this fact intuitively as she opened the Williams Career School of Excellence. She and her husband aim to equip their students with skills that empower them to establish economic stability, which will also have a generational impact. The success of their graduates is proof that their efforts work.

Lora experienced a traumatic childhood without the benefit of a strong family support system. By the age of sixteen, she behaved in a way that was not healthy and not constructive for her future. She "mistakenly" signed up for Job Corps training and was surprised when she received a phone call notifying her that she had been selected. She considered the opportunity, believing that this must be divine intervention meant to lift her out of a dark place in her life. At this low point in her life, she struggled with indecision considering

"There are no accidents in life."

131

her life and her options. She believed that if she did not leave home, she would not live. A conversation with God gave her the strength to make the decision to leave. The decision to leave home at a young age was frightening, but she believes that this move was what saved her life and set her on a course for success.

Lora moved to San Marcos, Texas, to join the Job Corps. As the oldest child in her family, she felt a strong sense of responsibility. She had misgivings about leaving her siblings, but she knew that God whispered for her to "go." She was trained by the Job Corps for thirteen months and received Certified Nursing Assistant training. A one-on-one conversation with a favorite instructor during a challenging period in her training caused Lora to reassess some of her less-than-wise life choices. She encouraged Lora to believe in herself and her faith and encouraged her to trust that God had a plan for her. This was Lora's turning point.

After completing Job Corps training, Lora started her career as a CNA. She was also fortunate to meet her future husband, one of the associate pastors in her church. Now with a hunger for knowledge, Lora wanted to continue her education. She enrolled in Austin Community College to earn her Certified Medical Assistant (CMA) degree and certification. She loved her position as CNA/CMA working with the elderly in an assisted living residence but believed she might be able to effect changes more in this environment if she had an advanced Licensed Vocational Nurse (LVN) or Registered Nurse (RN) credential. Back to school the avid learner went. After receiving her LVN degree, she was promoted into management as a supervisor, where she was confident she could improve the quality of care in residential communities. As she worked full time in management, she also continued her education

and ultimately received her RN designation. Even though studies show that only 20% of individuals with a CNA go on to achieve the LVN license and only 10% continue to receive the RN degree within six years, Lora has beaten the odds. She has done both. With the encouragement of her husband and her trust that she was on the path that God had for her, she grew in knowledge and confidence.

A decade prior to becoming an RN, Lora and her husband dreamed of starting their own businesses. She believed that through journaling, reflection and prayer she would discern the perfect direction for her talents and her service. Because of her reliance on her conversations with God, her trust in the process and faith that the right path would be revealed, she was confident when she received the message to launch a training center (which has become the Williams Career School of Excellence). The school's goal was to prepare students for certified nursing assistant careers. These nurses would be of service in a way that honored the special needs of the elderly. Along with providing education, WCSE also helps students graduate debt-free from the program by offering affordable tuition and payment plans. Many of Lora's students do not feel that college is the path for them. With WCSE, Lora created a program that was not only instructive but also transformative, providing central Texas students and their families with a path toward economic stability.

During the early months of 2020, with a global pandemic affecting education, Lora knew that she could develop a hybrid training program for WCSE with the majority of the training in an online platform. Lora developed this new type of successful CNA training program and now consults with other educational groups who want to emulate her success in their programs.

Along with her role as head of the WCSE school, she also is an author, a philanthropist and a motivational speaker. Her inspirational books, *Passionately Pursued by Love, Woman Arise, I Believe You, Little One* and *Renewed* are meant to provide tools and principles based on the word of God to ignite hope with the lives of readers. Her philanthropy includes giving back to Gary Job Corps Center, youth organizations in Africa, and local groups that encourage empowerment in women. She is a servant, a giver and an advocate.

Lora's first introduction to Black Women in Business was through a vendor opportunity to share her books. Once she became aware of the organization, she learned how powerful the community is. The organization has paved the way for more learning. Through the connections she made in BWIB, she became aware that there were many Black women doing incredible things, running businesses and demonstrating that women are powerful forces within the community and in their families. Lora has seen the advantages to the business education, the camaraderie and the support of her fellow business owners. There is a lot of power in knowing that the members aren't going it alone.

As a consultant to other educational businesses and as an inspirational speaker, Lora advises women who might be considering starting a business to take the step and do it. She credits her strong faith in God for providing the resilience needed to grow from a frightened child with little hope for the future to a woman with a successful career as an entrepreneur, author and speaker. Obedience to working the plan, listening to God and believing in herself are what she wishes for all those who look to her as an example.

I NOW GIVE MYSELF
PERMISSION TO LIVE
A BIG LIFE.

I WILL STEP INTO WHO
I AM MEANT TO BE.

I WILL STOP PLAYING SMALL.

I AM MEANT FOR
GREATER THINGS.

INTRODUCTION

`*Guinness Book of World Records*, Accessed August 23, 2022, https://www. guinnessworldrecords.com/world-records/first-self-made-millionairess.

Emily Donahue, David Brown, "Austin's the Only Fast-Growing City in the Country Losing African-Americans." May 16, 2014, KUT 90.5, https://www.kut.org/austin/2014-05-16/ austins-the-only-fast-growing-city-in-the-country-losing-african-americans.

TANISHA BARNETT

Soulaima Gourani, "Why Most Women Give Up on Their Dreams." Forbes, July 29, 2019, https://www.forbes.com/sites/soulaimagourani/2019/07/29/ why-most-women-give-up-on-their-dreams/.

Benedict Clark, "How Much Does a Website Increase Sales?" Acquire.io, Updated January 18, 2022, https://acquire.io/blog/how-much-does-a-website-increase-sales/.

DR. KERRIE CARTER-WALKER

Lilah Koski, "The Side Hustle Gender Gap." EllevateNetwork.com, Accessed July 20, 2022, https://www.ellevatenetwork.com/articles/9878-the-side-hustle-gender-gap.

BINI

Simple Truths, "212 The Extra Degree: Extraordinary Results Begin with One Small Change." YouTube, June 3, 2009, 2:50, https://youtu.be/NPEeEqkEjAQ.

SIANNI DEAN

Jennifer Kuadli, "Women Entrepreneurs Statistics." February 2, 2021, https://legaljobs.io/blog/women-entrepreneurs-statistics/.

SONYA HOWARD

Editorial Staff, "Franchise Statistics." July 1, 2022, https://appsthatdeliver.com/insights/franchise-statistics.

Wendy Sawyer, "Prisons and Jails Will Separate Millions of Mothers from Their Children in 2022." Prison Policy Initiative, May 4, 2022, https://www.prisonpolicy.org/blog/2022/05/04/mothers_day/.

Franchise Business REVIEW, "Should You Buy a Franchise or Start a Business From Scratch?" July 19, 2018, https://franchisebusinessreview.com/post/buy-a-franchise-vs-start-business-from-scratch/.

KIMBERLY (KIMBER) MCCARVER

Beth Moore, "Blogging Benefits Mental Health & Holistic Wellness." November 1, 2018, https://moorewellness.life/blogging-benefits-mental-health.

Adeel Qayum, "How to Start a Skincare Line: the Ultimate Guide for 2022." January 31, 2022, https://www.oberlo.com/blog/how-to-start-a-skincare-line.

YVETTE MCGILL

Darius Cikanavicius, "How Lack of Love in Childhood Robs Us of Love in Adulthood." PsychCentral, September 30, 2019, https://psychcentral.com/blog/psychology-self/2019/09/trauma-lack-of-love#1.

REFERENCES

KATII MCKINNEY

Dragomir Simovic, "39 Entrepreneur Statistics You Need to Know in 2022." SmallBizGenius, February 25, 2022, https://www.smallbizgenius.net/by-the-numbers/entrepreneur-statistics/.

PATRICIA (PAT) MOORE

Oberlo, "How Many People Shop Online in 2022?" Accessed July 20, 2022, https://www.oberlo.com/statistics/how-many-people-shop-online.

Nick Perry, "Brick-and-Mortar Stores vs Online Stores Statistics [2022]." Fundera.com, Updated December 21, 2021, https://www.fundera.com/resources/brick-and-mortar-vs-online-statistics.

Oberlo, "How Many People Shop Online in 2022." Access August 23, 2022, https://www.oberlo.com/statistics/how-many-people-shop-online.

NeuroTrackerX Team, "Why Shopping Makes you Feel High." December 18, 2016, https://www.neurotrackerx.com/post/shopping-makes-feel-high.

DINEEN PARKER

The Tab, "Dropping Out of College to Serve My Country Was the Best Decision I Ever Made," Accessed July 20, 2022, https://thetab.com/us/2017/06/27/dropping-out-of-college-69929.

Marina Pasquali, "Number of Active Etsy Sellers From 2012 – 2021." April 29, 2022, https://www.statista.com/statistics/409374/etsy-active-sellers/.

SHIRLEY QUICK

Tanner Christensen, "Childhood Role Models and Their Influence on Creativity." CreativeSomething.net, January 8, 2018, https://creativesomething.net/post/2017/12/7/childhood-role-models-and-their-influence-on-creativity.

SHARON SMITH

Chimene Richa, MD, "These Are the Health Risks of Having a BMI Over 30." January 15, 2020, https://ro.co/health-guide/health-risks-of-obesity/.

LORA WILLIAMS

Iris Palmer, "We need to fix the broken nursing career pathway—here's how." NewAmerica.org, April 5, 2021, https://www.newamerica.org/education-policy/edcentral/we-need-to-fix-the-broken-nursing-career-pathwayheres-how/.

Neeraj Kaushal, "Intergenerational Payoffs of Education." *Future Child* 24, no. 1 (Spring 2014): 61–78, doi: 10.1353. https://pubmed.ncbi.nlm.nih.gov/25518703/.

Acknowledgments

IT IS IMPOSSIBLE TO THANK EVERY PERSON that has invested in my life and poured into my soul. My journey has been filled with amazing family members, friends, colleagues and beautiful strangers that came along just when I needed a breath of fresh air. The Black Women In Business journey has been a challenging yet rewarding one. It has proved that we are better together. I am grateful for you all.

The completion of this book would not have been possible without the support of my husband Charles Smith, my daughter, Delissa Chase, my son, Debrico Chase, my nephew, Avery Chase and Black Women In Business Executive Director, Briana Murphy. Thank you for coming to my rescue and giving me the time needed to write during one of the most challenging times of my life. Your love, support and encouragement will never be forgotten. Love you all...

Rose Smith

All creative efforts start with an idea. As Elizabeth Gilbert writes, "New ideas seek a home. And unless we allow our ideas to take hold, they will go away and look for someone else to bring them to life." The idea to share the stories and wisdom of an amazing group of resilient members of Black Women in Business in Austin, Texas, found its home in the co-authors' collaboration. We are so grateful to the many individuals who lent a hand in bringing our book to life. The dream team of Amy Collette, Alexandra O'Connell and Victoria Wolf worked diligently to bring the stories to the page. Tim Babiak and David Coleman provided imagination and photographic support to showcase the authenticity in each woman's face. And innumerable friends and family provided support and space to get the writing completed in a record amount of time. Finally, sending bundles of admiration for the women who get the job done every day with grit and grace and resilience.

Deborah Cole

About the Authors

ROSE SMITH

Rose Smith is the award-winning CEO of Black Women in Business, which has ten Texas Chapters. She is a motivational speaker, author, brand and success coach. She is known to her members and community as Coach Rose, and her mission is to "change the game."

She is the creator and organizer of the COVID Community Food Relief Program, established in March 2020. Black Women In Business has provided free groceries to 95,000 families with no governmental funding. In 2021, BWIB invested food and personal products exceeding $1,000,000 into the community. She says this program is a tremendous display of community unity, and a perfect example of what can be accomplished when we work together.

Mrs. Smith received the 2022 I Am Austin Woman award, and Mayor Steve Adler proclaimed August 2, 2022, Coach Rose Chase Smith Day.

DEBORAH COLE

Deborah Cole is a speaker and author who leads first from the heart. Armed with a graduate degree from Texas A&M University, she founded and led a commercial landscape company with branches throughout the State of Texas, employing over 500 team members. During her thirty-five years as president, Deborah discovered and supported a next generation of leaders who successfully took the reins of the company when it became employee-owned in 2008. Since 2017, she has focused full time on writing, speaking and consulting.

Whether growing her business to the top 25 list in the U.S. in her industry, receiving honors in business or serving on boards, she uses her writing, speaking and people-centric photography to inspire and educate. She has had photos in juried exhibitions in Texas and New York. She has created text and images for two books, "Letting Go: How Less Becomes More" (2020) and "She: Believed She Could So She Did" (2022).

Deborah has been awarded top honors in Austin's Profiles in Power, with her company being named one of the Best Places to Work by the Austin Business Journal. She has served as Contributor or Editor for numerous regional and national publications and has been honored by state organizations as an outstanding volunteer. She served as the first President of the Texas Association of Landscape Contractors and currently holds a leadership role in the Women in Landscape Network and is a member of the Council of Diversity, Equity and Inclusion for the National Association of Landscape Contractors.